P9-DGT-137

PRAISE FOR *Rise of the Youpreneur*

"In six years, I've built an eight-figure, personal brand business. If I had read *Rise of the Youpreneur* before I started I could have done it in half the time. Your mileage may vary, but one thing is clear: if you want to build a business based on your personal brand, there's no better time than now—and there is no better guide than Chris Ducker."

MICHAEL HYATT
New York Times bestselling author of *Your Best Year Ever*

"Timely, relevant, and powerful, *Rise of the Youpreneur* is the instruction manual for building a thriving personal brand business. Recommended!"

JAY BAER
Founder of Convince & Convert and author of *Hug Your Haters*

"In today's world, building a personal brand is not as hard as it used to be. However, becoming a profitable personal brand entrepreneur is not as easy. In *Rise of the Youpreneur*, Chris Ducker serves up the strategies you need to help you achieve exactly that and beyond."

MICHAEL PORT
New York Times and *Wall Street Journal* bestselling author of *Steal the Show*

"I've been an entrepreneur for over 10 years now. I think I have this thing figured out, but I still listen to every word Chris Ducker says. His guidance always helps me to focus on what's important. He'll do the same for you with this book."

JOE PULIZZI
Bestselling author of *Content Inc.*

"In *Rise of the Youpreneur*, successful serial entrepreneur Chris Ducker declares that a personal brand business is the last career pivot you'll ever need to make. He's right. We're all entrepreneurs now. Follow the guidance in this book and you will learn exactly how to design a lifestyle and a living you love, one that can grow and evolve as exponentially and dynamically as you do."

JENNY BLAKE
Author of PIVOT: The Only Move That Matters Is Your Next One

"This is it. The book every entrepreneur who wants to build a personal brand needs to read—from a fellow entrepreneur who truly knows what he's talking about. Nobody knows this stuff better than Chris Ducker."

JEFF GOINS
Bestselling author of *Real Artists Don't Starve*

"It takes courage to commit to yourself, but courage is not enough. It also takes smarts, so you can rise above the clamor and ensure the right people become your fans and your customers. Chris Ducker's *Rise of the Youpreneur* is the right way to get braver and smarter about making a splash."

MICHAEL BUNGAY STAINER
Author of *Do More Great Work* and *The Coaching Habit*

"Chris has done it again in *Rise of the Youpreneur*! As a big believer in the value of a personal brand, I know what it takes to make it work for your business and this book delivers that roadmap. With actionable steps, invaluable perspective, and a little bit (okay, actually quite a lot!) of that Ducker flavor, I'll be recommending this resource to my community many times over."

AMY SCHMITTAUER LANDINO
Founder of Savvy Sexy Social and bestselling author of *Vlog Like a Boss*

"If you want a future-proof, recession-proof business that you can be proud of for your entire life, then you want to start working on YOU. In *Rise of the Youpreneur*, Ducker gives you the only playbook you'll ever need. Mandatory reading for my clients and my kids!"

MATTHEW KIMBERLEY
Bestselling author of *How to Get a Grip*

"There are thousands of guys running around telling you how to be an entrepreneur. But Ducker is different. He speaks not only from experience, but also from the heart. He tells you what works and what doesn't work, and he does so with a care and compassion that can only come from someone who's been in the trenches, who's made mistakes, and who's come out stronger on the other side. This is the book I wish I'd had when I started my entrepreneurial journey, twenty years ago."

PETER SHANKMAN
Founder of Help a Reporter Out (HARO) and author of *Zombie Loyalists*

"In an increasingly noisy online world, your personal brand can be the most effective way to reach people with your message and build a sustainable business for the long term. *Rise of the Youpreneur* will help you identify the key elements that will help you stand out, and show you how to authentically share your story to attract fans, and customers, over time. Chris Ducker has created an online empire around his own brand, and in this book he shares how you can do it yourself."

JOANNA PENN
New York Times and *USA Today* bestselling author at TheCreativePenn.com

"This book is relevant, genuine, and full of heart! I'd expect nothing less from the amazing Chris Ducker. Find yourself a cosy little nook and shut off your smartphone. Spend time with

Chris and bring out the Youpreneur you've always dreamed of becoming."

JOEL COMM
New York Times bestselling author of *Twitter Power*

"Chris does the important work of connecting the dots between solid business fundamentals and the unique personal power available to us in the digital age."

MARK SCHAEFER
Author of KNOWN: *Building & Unleashing Your Personal Brand in the Digital Age*

"In today's highly connected world, the best way to stand out as an entrepreneur is to build a compelling personal brand. In his new book, Chris helps fellow entrepreneurs tell their own personal stories, which lead toward new business conversations and relationships."

DAN SCHAWBEL
New York Times bestselling author of *Promote Yourself*

"As a Youpreneur, you find your path to success through your personal brand. In this snappy, motivating, and easy-to-read book, Chris Ducker shows you how to develop your personal brand by being different and memorable."

ANITA CAMPBELL
Founder and CEO of Small Business Trends

"The entrepreneurial world is full of copycats—everyone wants to be like someone else, but just a little quicker or cheaper. *Rise of the Youpreneur* exposes the futility of that thinking. True success embraces authenticity, generosity, and loving relationships. You can shine by being an original. This book will show you how 'being different is better than being better.'"

DAN MILLER
New York Times bestselling author of *48 Days to the Work You Love*

"Chris Ducker has lived a lot of the stories that other people talk about in theory. *Rise of the Youpreneur* is stuffed full of the advice you need. Dig in."

CHRIS BROGAN
CEO of Owner Media Group

"Chris Ducker is the person I've always turned to for advice when deciding the direction to take my business. He is a branding genius and the person we should all be asking 'what's next' in the exciting world we live in. Thanks to Chris, the 'brand' John Lee Dumas is on fire, and I look forward to learning from him for decades to come!"

JOHN LEE DUMAS
Founder and Host of *Entrepreneurs on Fire*

"If you're someone who aspires to break the mold and tread your own path, carry this guide on your journey to success."

MICHAEL STELZNER
Founder of Social Media Examiner

"Chris doesn't just know the formula for building a long-term, successful business; he lives and practices it, too. His passion for helping others find and utilize their superpowers to make a living is unmatched, and I'm stoked that he's now written *Rise of the Youpreneur*—the ultimate guide for personal business success."

PAT FLYNN
Wall Street Journal bestselling author of *Will It Fly?*

"Throughout the pages of *Rise of the Youpreneur*, Chris Ducker cuts through all the noise and nonsense around 'personal branding' and delivers what you truly need to know and do to build a viable business that's based on your unique personality and strengths."

BRIAN CLARK
Founder of Copyblogger.com and CEO of Rainmaker Digital

"Your experience, skills, style, and story make you your best asset. There is absolutely no one better to teach you how to leverage all of that into a powerful business than Chris Ducker. I recommend this book, his business, his events, and his coaching to everyone I know looking to build an online brand, because I trust him. Chris challenges me personally every time I read his material, listen to his podcast, or hear him speak. Heed his advice. I always do."

CARRIE WILKERSON
Speaker and author of *The Barefoot Executive*

"I have watched Chris Ducker over the last decade go from strength to strength, which is why I'm so excited about his latest book, *Rise of the Youpreneur.* Now, for the first time, Chris is sharing all his secrets and how you too can build a dream business. Own it and read it. You'll be glad you did."

DALE BEAUMONT
Founder and CEO of Business Blueprint and BRiN.ai

"There is only one way to remove the risks associated with becoming an entrepreneur and that's to pour all of yourself into becoming the most sought after resource on your business planet—Rise Up, Youpreneurs!"

JOHN JANTSCH
Bestselling author of *Duct Tape Marketing*

"The best part of this book is that before he wrote it, Chris Ducker lived it for decades, proving that a personal brand business is future-proof in the way no entrepreneur or business model has been before. There's no better time to 'rise' than now!"

AMY PORTERFIELD
Host of the *Online Marketing Made Easy* podcast

RISE OF THE YOUPRENEUR

CHRIS DUCKER

RISE OF THE YOUPRENEUR

The Definitive Guide to Becoming
the Go-To Leader in Your Industry and
Building a Future-Proof Business

4C
PRESS

4C Press
Cambridge UK
www.4cpress.com

ISBN 978-1-9998579-4-3 (paperback)
ISBN 978-1-9998579-1-2 (limited edition paperback)
ISBN 978-1-9998579-0-5 (hardcover)
ISBN 978-1-9998579-2-9 (ebook)
IBSN 978-1-9998579-3-6 (audiobook)

Produced by Page Two
www.pagetwostrategies.com
Cover and interior design by Peter Cocking

This book is dedicated to entrepreneurs just like YOU, who have dared to stand out from the crowd and do things your own special way.

The impact you're making on the world is greater than you'll ever know.

CONTENTS

FOREWORD

REMEMBER so clearly the day I realized I could make money—real money. I was a young hustler, working my butt off day in and day out, trying to figure out how to make more than a few hundred dollars doing what I enjoyed. I'd spent months building up a decent reputation as "The LinkedIn Guy" back in 2009 and was known for throwing big networking events. I was making some money, but I was exhausted and couldn't figure out how to scale.

Then I met a guy who *had* figured out how to make money. He had a huge audience and invited me to join a webinar he was hosting and teach LinkedIn strategies to the attendees. I didn't really know what a webinar was at the time, but I saw it as a major opportunity and said yes.

When the webinar day arrived, I was so nervous that I took off my shirt because I was stress-sweating through it. Thankfully, no webcams were expected back then, so no one knew! I fumbled over my words, hurried through my amateur slides, and then finally remembered that I knew what I was talking about on the subject of LinkedIn. I found my groove and delivered some quality content. At the end of my presentation, I threw up my personal PayPal link and offered a $150 Advanced LinkedIn Bootcamp for anyone who wanted to learn more.

The webinar ended, and I nervously left my laptop alone because I was scared I would somehow mess it up (even though it was already done). Finally, I decided it was safe to check my email in case anyone had actually bought the program.

When I checked out my inbox, I almost cried. It was the most beautiful thing I'd ever seen. My inbox was full of messages, and they all said the same thing: "You've received a payment from..."

I couldn't believe it, so I logged into my PayPal account and saw $6,200 sitting in it! I lost my mind, screamed with joy, danced around in my underwear, and was so excited I didn't care what the neighbors thought about me, as they must've seen me in the window!

I had finally figured out how to make real money!

With that single experience, it all clicked. I started to understand what making money online was all about. It was simply a matter of sharing my specific personality and expertise with an eager, curious audience.

Fast-forward eight years, and my business has grown beyond what I could have imagined. I'm a *New York Times* bestselling author, a premier keynote speaker, the host of a podcast that is listened to by millions of fans around the world, and the sole owner of a multiple-seven-figures-a-year business that I love. And the best part is, I still feel like I'm just getting started!

This has been possible only because of what I learned that day on the sweaty webinar: how to make sustainable, large profits with my unique skill set and personality. It's the lesson that has transformed thousands of business owners from workaholic, stressed-out entrepreneurs into successful, impactful, *joyful* game changers.

Chris is one of the finest examples of this transformation that I know. I met him years ago, when I was still molding my brand and finding my voice. He taught me about the importance of delegation, team-building, personal branding, and how to create a sustainable entrepreneurial lifestyle.

I immediately trusted him and took his advice: he was practicing what he preached, and I could see the freedom and results he had in his life. From running a huge bricks-and-mortar company that had completely burned him out to building a business that supports his unique skills, experience, and personality, he was the living proof that personal branding makes everything possible.

I've turned to him so many times through the years to get advice on my own business, run ideas by him, and stay grounded on this wild ride of entrepreneurship. I can easily say that he gets it like few do.

The truth, as Seth Godin says, is that we're in a relationship economy, and customers want to buy from people they know and trust. That means we have a responsibility to show who we are, what our mission is, and how we are moving toward it. We get to show our true colors. We get to own our voices. We get to reveal that we're human, committed to learning and being better. That's when our audiences will automatically connect with us.

That's when they'll choose *us* over every other option they have.

As I look to the future and how the world's economies are evolving, I know this for sure: building a business based on a personal brand that is focused on service to others is a sure way to succeed as an entrepreneur in the long run.

Join us on the road. There's room for everyone.

LEWIS HOWES

New York Times Bestselling Author

Top 100 Podcast in the World: *The School of Greatness*

INTRODUCTION

STARTED my first business in a very different world.

Back then, in 2004, the best advice out there was to stay out of my business's way. I was supposed to be the architect behind the scenes, the hidden puppet master. There was no one out there acting as the very public face of their brands—or, at least, *almost* no one—and as a result, most businesses were exclusively about the service or product they offered.

Fast-forward to 2010. I'd launched two more successful companies, and there's no denying that the old advice had continued to work. I'd not only built a successful business-processing firm, as well as a co-working space, but my third business, a remote staffing hub, continues to serve customers all over the world every day.

The only problem was that the effort to start each new business was Herculean, to say the least. Every new business meant I would spend years building, marketing, and monetizing from the ground up, and even when I'd done it before, I had to start from scratch for every new company. If you've been in this position, or thought about starting a business, you know what I mean.

That was also the year that more and more entrepreneurs started blogging and podcasting as a way of sharing what they knew. *Why not try it out?* I ventured. By then, I'd been in the game long enough to know I had some insights to share. I didn't know who would tune in, but to someone like me who thrives on a challenge and the chance to bring people together, the growing world of online community-building was irresistible.

Little did I know that this simple "side hustle" would soon change the rules of business altogether—for me and for everyone else.

Within just a few years of blogging and podcasting regularly, I'd reached several professional milestones that had never been possible when I was behind the scenes:

- My audience grew globally by tens of thousands.
- I'd keynoted big-stage events all over the world.
- People wanted to hire me to coach and mentor them.
- I launched and sold out year after year a premium-ticket, destination mastermind retreat in the tropics.
- I received four offers to publish my first book, *Virtual Freedom*, which, when launched, quickly became an Amazon bestseller with over 800 five-star reviews.

What made such exponential growth possible in just two years? In retrospect, I can see quite clearly how closely everything correlates to the EXACT time I stopped following the old rules of business. I came out from behind the curtain, took center stage, and began to attract a global audience that cared about more than just the product or service I offered. They cared about being part of my community and being supported in their own efforts to build, market, and monetize their ventures.

They wanted to follow along with my journey and share their own.

I know now that 2010 was the year I launched my personal brand, before I even knew what that was or what it meant. It's turned out to be one of the best moves I ever made in my career.

Enter the Youpreneur

In late 2014, I coined the term *Youpreneur* to describe the rise of the personal brand entrepreneur and a new business model that very few people saw coming.

A Youpreneur transcends the old rules of business and builds a sustainable and lasting business from the foundation of their experience, interests, and personality... ultimately, their personal brand.

A Youpreneur IS the very public face of their business, and they draw an engaged, loyal audience even as they pursue varying, changing interests. Think Sir Richard Branson, Elon Musk, Jeff Bezos, and Gary Vaynerchuk. These Youpreneurs can and DO pursue everything they're interested in, and their communities follow along eagerly.

A Youpreneur leverages the timelessness of their personality and unique experience to lead and grow with their audiences despite changing economies, shifting technologies, and uncertain circumstances.

Youpreneurs play by their own rules, and if you're ready to join the movement, you'll notice two huge benefits, both immediately and going forward:

1. A personal brand business is the last pivot you'll ever need to make.

Like I said, I'm used to building businesses from the ground up. I've done it for myself multiple times, and I've personally coached hundreds of others through the same process. It's a lot of work, and it can be dispiriting to think that if you ever want to try a different business down the road, you'll have to start all over again. If you've yet to build your first business, it can be daunting to wonder how long it'll last before market trends demand you pivot, sell, or start again.

With a personal brand business, however, the only and final business you have to build is The Business of You. You're free to pursue all your professional interests under the umbrella of being a Youpreneur, and a change in interests doesn't mean losing all the work you've already put into building, marketing, and monetizing.

Establishing my personal brand has meant that all my interests, even as they change, are still part of the Chris Ducker brand, and that my audience follows me as I pursue, explore, develop, and share those interests. If I want to talk about entrepreneurship one day and travel the next, I can do that because my business isn't about any one product or service. It's about me and the people I serve, just as your Youpreneur business will be about you and the people you serve.

2. The Youpreneur business model is future-proof.

This is where it gets really exciting.

Everything I've observed and experienced as a Youpreneur confirms that personal brand businesses are future-proof in the way no entrepreneur, or business model, has been before.

Think about it: when your business is focused only on a service or product you provide, customers have little incentive to stay loyal. They'll jump ship for the next-lowest price if all they have to compare is deliverables.

But Youpreneurs know better than that. For us, business is about relationships, and relationships inspire loyalty, generosity, and service in an infinite loop.

It's this mindset that will help you become the go-to source—the go-to leader in your market.

People want to do business with other people. Youpreneurs make sure their audiences know them as people, and as a direct result, they have none of the external constraints and worries that product- or service-focused businesses do. As a Youpreneur, no matter what happens in the world, outside forces can't control or dictate what your business does, how much money you can make, or how big an impact you can have.

You're in full control, and the future is always bright.

Now, make no mistake, launching The Business of You is still a huge undertaking. It requires the same enormous effort as starting any business, but the facts are that it's the last pivot you'll ever have to make, and you'll be future-proofing yourself and your success going forward.

This book will walk you through the exact process I followed when shifting from entrepreneur to Youpreneur myself. It's the same process I've walked literally thousands of students and coaching clients through as they've made the switch themselves. You can read step-by-step, building your business with every page, and you'll come out the other side with a solid personal brand and proven "Youpreneur ecosystem" that'll sustain you and those who you desire to serve for years to come.

Ready to rise and future-proof your business as a Youpreneur?

Good.

Let's get started!

A PERSONAL INVITATION

BEFORE we officially get started, I've got some good news for you.

Regardless of how long you've been at "this" (whatever your "this" is!), the chances are you're probably further along in your growth as an entrepreneur than you think.

However, the biggest problem I see entrepreneurs facing when it comes to kick-starting The Business of You model is that they don't know what to focus on at the start.

And the "start" is different for everyone. Why? Because we're all at different stages of growth.

To counter this, I'd like to invite you to take the Youpreneur "Next Step" Assessment. It's a simple online assessment that will help you discover how far along you are in your journey, but more importantly, it'll help you figure out what your next move should be.

Taking the assessment is essential for truly getting to grips with the content throughout this book.

Together, we'll determine where you're currently at in the *Build, Market, Monetize* process, and how I can best support your growth going forward.

Answer each question honestly, and be prepared to be surprised about where you are and where you're yet to go. This is a journey, and an exciting one at that—and if you're reading this, you're ready to get started... and I'm ready to help you every step of the way.

Visit **Youpreneur.com/NextStep** and let's chase it down... together!

PART 1
BUILDING

1

DEFINING
WHO YOU ARE

YOUR Youpreneur journey starts right now. I like to think of it as an intentional effort to build a brand that connects your business to a message your audience will be able to find, understand, and relate to.

One of the biggest mistakes I see entrepreneurs make is that they never figure out how to define their business. This can make it almost impossible to build a successful brand and, consequently, a profitable business over the long term.

Becoming a Youpreneur means you won't make that mistake. You will define what you and your business are all about—right out of the gate. This understanding will be your foundation as you build. Knowing who you are will enable you to truly captivate your audience.

Every journey has to start somewhere. And this one starts with you.

Know Yourself Inside and Out

Your story is your business. The very center of your business is sharing what you have done and can do for other people.

To do that successfully, you've got to think about your story and how to tell it in a way that people will relate to. You don't know how they may first encounter you. They may come to hear you speak and be right in front of you, or they may tune in on a podcast or find you through an Internet search or a social media mention. However or wherever people first meet you, you want them to connect with you in a deep and personal way, and to do this they must have access to the very core of what you are all about—your story.

- What have you done thus far?
- Where has your experience led you?
- What big milestones have you achieved in your career?
- Are you a family person?
- Are you all about the hustle and the grind?
- Do you happily work 18 hours a day or get it all done in just six?
- What do you do for fun?

All these things make up who you are and define you very clearly as an individual.

The best way to become a Youpreneur is to really be YOU 120 percent of the time. There's no room for smoke and mirrors. There're no funny games to be played. You've got to be you all the time.

The whole deal with really being you is that you will end up ultimately figuring out

- What you're all about.
- Who your perfect customer is.
- What you're going to sell them.

- How you're going to be marketing to them.
- What price point your offerings will be at.

Once you know all this, you will end up marketing like a magnet. And if you embrace the concept of "marketing like a magnet," you will do two things incrementally at the same time:

1. You will attract the perfect customer your way.
2. You will repel the people who shouldn't be on your radar in the first place.
   You've got to attract the best and repel the rest.

It's All About Trust

Trust is the single most important factor when it comes to business, period. If people don't trust you, they're not going to do business with you. **It's really that simple.** People want to do business with other people, not with other businesses or companies. That's true more so today than ever before in the history of business.

You hear a lot of talk about how someone has to "know, like, and trust" you before they'll end up doing business with you. But I think about it a little differently. I don't think it's know, like, and trust. It's actually know, *love*, and trust. Liking someone isn't enough anymore. I like a lot of people, but that doesn't necessarily mean that I'm going to end up parting with my money just because we're acquainted.

What you need to do is ultimately become somebody's favorite—whether it's favorite business coach, wellness coach, blogger, podcaster, vlogger, speaker, or author.

Your goal should be to become somebody's favorite.

Trust plays such a massively important role in that process because, at the end of the day, beyond our own weird and

You've got to **attract** the best and **repel** the rest.

warped opinions, we tend to believe the opinions of other people around us—the people we trust.

And this has a ripple effect.

You're not going to believe someone you've just met on the subway over somebody that you've known and who's been in your circle for years and years. So, you want to become a favorite, you want to be LOVED, and you want to be trusted.

As important as it is to build trust with your audience, you have to always remember that trust is a fragile thing. It can take forever to build and only a second, or one bad decision, to destroy.

When building your story, you want to be as honest as possible in everything. The world we live in today is a very social world—a very online and connected world—so if you tell porky pies, as we say in London, you will be found out. You can't just make something up or embellish the truth. If you do, you will be found out; there's absolutely no doubt about it. It might not happen this week, this month, this year, or this decade, but sooner or later, you are going to be called out on it.

In that moment, the trust you worked so hard to develop will be gone in a flash. This is nothing new. You've been told not to lie since you can remember—actually, humans have been told this since the beginning of time. After all, it's one of the 10 Commandments, right? And yet, dishonesty is still one of the most crippling factors in business today.

Honesty should be at the very core of what you are all about. You must be truthful and represent yourself and your business to the people you want to serve in a manner that shows them admiration and respect.

Being an Original

When building The Business of You, being different is everything.

But being original can boost your business faster than anything. The fact is we do business in a very, very, very crowded space nowadays. It is almost impossible to come up with a 100 percent original business idea or a 100 percent original marketing concept.

Unfortunately, the entry barrier to calling yourself an entrepreneur and an original is at an all-time low. You can pretty much say anything you want online about yourself or your business, and for the most part, people will believe it. The other problem, and perhaps a larger one, is that people are just blatantly copying each other. I'm the first one to call people out on this.

I don't feel like you need to copy somebody to launch a product, or to market your blog or your podcast, or to get speaking gigs, or to put together a book. You can get inspiration from other people's work. You can watch what your competitors are doing. But ultimately success will come down to you and how you want to be talked about when you're not around.

I've been on conference stages all around the world, key-noting to hundreds and hundreds of people, and have shown examples on the screen of people blatantly copying each other. I call people out publicly. It's not just because I've been a victim of copyright infringement; it is simply a sloppy way to build your business. You shouldn't just be looking to do something better than your competitors. You should be looking to do something different.

At the end of the day, being different is a far easier way to be remembered than simply being better than your competitors.

At the end of the day, when we talk about being original and remaining original, you are the biggest difference. When you build The Business of You, it is 100 percent original because there is only one of you in existence. The persona of your business can't be copied because it's all about

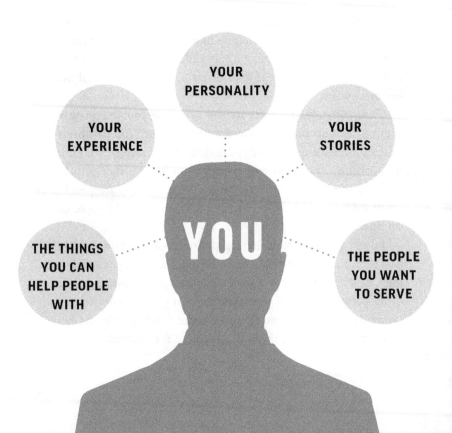

YOUR PERSONALITY

YOUR EXPERIENCE

YOUR STORIES

THE THINGS YOU CAN HELP PEOPLE WITH

YOU

THE PEOPLE YOU WANT TO SERVE

At the end of the day, **being different** is a far easier way to **be remembered** than simply being better than your competitors.

Remember, remaining original all comes down to just being you all the time. This is why I said earlier that a smoke-and-mirrors act doesn't work. Sooner or later, you will trip up and be left with egg on your face.

In order to show up externally, you have to know who you are internally. This is about telling your story. That has to start with knowing who you are completely as a person. You always hear people talk about trying to find themselves or that they can't figure out who they want to be.

This, really, is about you becoming you.

Here's what my close friend and entrepreneurial ally Pat Flynn says in his book *Will It Fly?*: "The world needs you. It needs your energy and what you have to offer."

So, the first question you've really got to ask yourself is, what makes you great? What will make you stand out from the crowd? This self-awareness should be at the top of every Youpreneur's must-have list in regards to skill set. It's so important to figure out what makes you great. The flip side of that coin is that you've got to be real with yourself. You've got to be acutely aware of what you struggle with. You'll want to highlight the positives, obviously.

This, really, is about you **becoming** you.

The Youpreneur Self-Awareness Test

There's an exercise I get my coaching clients to do when I'm helping them to know themselves. Take a piece of paper and draw a line down the middle. On one side of that line, write down all the things you believe that you're great at. I call this the "flatter yourself" list. You've got to really pat yourself on the back and make yourself sound amazing, because you are!

Let's say, for example, you're a wellness coach. You might list something like understanding how to dig deep into your customers' biggest triggers for pain or stress. That skill would make you great as a wellness coach. Other examples could be the ability to assess people's medical records and understand where they are before and after you work with them, or the ability to get people to accept new routines that incorporate fitness, stress management, and meditation. All the things that a wellness coach should be adept at doing.

If you're a business coach, your "flatter yourself" list will look very different. You may have skills like being able to read and understand a profit and loss statement. You'd be amazed how many business owners don't know how to read a P&L statement—myself included! For the first three years of my business, I didn't care about my bloody P&L statement! All I cared about was whether I was making money or not. Eventually, my financial director came up to me and said, "Boss, I think you should learn how to read this thing because we might be able to change things up a bit and save some money here and there." Lo and behold, she spent five hours with me one day walking me through a profit and loss statement so I really understood how to read it properly, and we started saving four or five percent of our costs each month after that. If you have the skill of helping your clients read their P&L statements, write it down! Your customers will love you for it.

Now, when you are done listing all the things you are great at, write the second list on the other side of that middle line. This one isn't quite as fun, but it's equally important, I promise.

This is the "let's be real" list, as I like to call it. These are all the things that you know you struggle with. I come across people who are not real about their weaknesses. I often say that if you are not a graphic designer—like, an actual real graphic designer—you have absolutely no right sitting in Photoshop trying to design a website logo or an image for social media. That stuff should be delegated. It's not worth your time to do things that you struggle with. You can find others who are good at those activities, and they will do it better and faster than you ever could. As a bonus, you will be able to focus on and accomplish the things you are good at—the things from your "flatter yourself" list!

Here's a look at a section of my very own Youpreneur Self-Awareness Test:

YOUPRENEUR SELF-AWARENESS TEST

Flatter Yourself	Let's Be Real
Strong Leader	Micro-Manager
Compelling Communicator	Perfectionist
High Achiever	Impatient
Competitive Drive	Tech Incompetent
Independent Worker	Easily Unimpressed

As you can see, one thing I still struggle with to this day is managing people. I'll be the first to admit I'm a pretty crappy manager, quite frankly. However, what I can do is lead people. I can lead people into whatever battle is in front of them. I'm a good leader, but I'm not a very good manager, so what do I do? I hire people who can manage people well. I hire people who can manage departments well so that I don't have to struggle through it myself.

This is the kind of self-awareness that every entrepreneur fights to achieve—or, worse, doesn't realize is important until they make a costly mistake! It can be an ongoing battle, but if you can figure out *A) what you do really, really well—what makes you great,* and *B) what you don't do so well—what you struggle with* as early as possible, it's going to set you up for higher levels of success in the future.

It's your job to make sure you're working with the people you can effect the most change for!

Authors, speakers, coaches, consultants, experts, workshop facilitators, seminar speakers, bloggers, podcasters, live streamers... these types of people (people like YOU!) were put on Earth to drop your "value bombs" from great heights. At the end of the day, there's nothing more relatable to your market than you. Once you define what you are all about, you can start building out your brand-based business.

Doing this at the beginning stages of your business planning is important because it defines the entire business model you'll be creating.

Understanding who you are and knowing yourself inside and out might not seem like it's relating or relatable to your market right now, but it will be further down the line. It will all come into play when it's time to understand your market and create content to serve them properly and answer their questions, so that they can get onto your email list and buy your products. Self-awareness is going to help you help them achieve a certain level of success before ever attending your workshops or live events and so on and so on.

This, right here, is everything!

When I help a client develop their business model, their products and services, or the experiences that they want to serve their audience with, I think about the end first.

You've probably heard of the term "begin with the end in mind."

It's 100 percent bang on.

It's your job to make sure you're working with the people you can effect the most change for!

Writing Your Business Obituary

One of my favorite things to do when I start working with a new coaching client is have them write their business obituary.

When I say we're going to start with the end in mind, I really mean THE END!

The question is, how do you want your business to be remembered when it's not around anymore? What kind of legacy do you want your business to have? When everything is said and done, when the clouds part, when the dust settles, whatever metaphors you want to use, when it's all finished, how do you want people to talk about you and the impact that you've had through your business? I am challenging you to write your business obituary right now!

Ask yourself not only how do I want my business to be remembered, but also what would I want people to say about it? You've really got to reach for the stars when you are doing this. Hold nothing back in any way whatsoever when writing this obituary.

This is like vision board stuff.

The Millennial crowd is all about creating vision boards. Not so long ago, we were in the process of buying a house, and my daughter Chloe said, "Dad, I'm working on vision boards." I had to ask her what the bloody hell a vision board was. She started showing me all these pictures of different living rooms, and another full set of different kitchen designs. She was envisioning how the living room would look when we were done furnishing it, and how the kitchen would look, how the bedroom would look, how the garden would look when we were done landscaping it.

She was dreaming up the perfect home for us.

This is what you need to do when it comes to your business obituary. Hold nothing back, reach for the stars, go all out.

- How much money did you make every year that your business was in business?
- How many lives did you change?
- How did you change them?
- How did your products and your services make your customers feel when they used them?

Because we're all familiar with Disney, I'm going to share my version of their business obituary here:

If Disney disappeared tomorrow, I would think of my first time ever at a Disney park. It was Disneyland in Los Angeles. This was five or six years ago. I remember queuing up because I didn't have the foresight to book tickets online.

I'm British, and one thing we Brits are good at is queuing up. In America, that's called "getting in line." I guess I liked the idea of queuing up for an hour in the heat of LA to buy tickets to enter a park. We get to the kiosk and, obviously, I'm not getting the online discounts, so I'm paying 20 percent more than what I would have if I'd just ordered the tickets online. I remember, quite explicitly, standing there with our three (at the time) kids and my wife—that's five of us in all—and I don't know exactly how much it cost now, but it was several hundred dollars. I remember turning to my wife and saying, "Good gosh, I haven't even gotten through the gates yet and they're already fleecing me."

I was instantly complaining about spending too much money. Then we went through those Disney gates to walk around and queue up at certain times for rides and shows. I didn't upgrade to the VIP ticket because I'm a bit of a tightarse, and that would have been way too efficient, anyway. Then we pay $20 for a burger and soda that would've cost $3 at McDonald's. Throughout the entire day, my first time there, I was kind of in complaining mode about the amount of money that I was spending.

Your brand is **what people say about you** when you are not at that dinner party, industry conference, coffee meeting, or networking event.

Oh, wait, now the kids are hot and sweaty, so what do we do? We purchase the little water bottle thingies with the fan. You press a button and it squirts water in your face. All these little "expenses" were building up throughout the day. But what I didn't realize was that experience after experience was building up as well. Throughout the entire day, it was one thing after another. Did we queue up 30 to 40 minutes just to get a photo with Mickey Mouse? Yes, but you should've seen my kids' eyes in that photo.

When my family left Disney that day, I looked at all the merchandise that I had purchased and reviewed all the junk that we'd eaten, and then I looked at all the smiles on my children's faces and on my wife's. As we walked out of the park, I actually had tears in my eyes, finally understanding just how important that first Disney experience was for us. We had such an incredible time.

To this day, Disney is one of my favorite companies on the planet. I can say that with confidence. Our entire household became lifelong fans that day at the park. Not to the point where I've got pictures of Mickey Mouse in my living room or anything like that, but my family feels connected to the ever-expanding universe of Disney, and we feel GREAT when we are there together, or even just remembering the great times we've had there in the past. How many times do you think we've gone back to Disney parks? We've gone to Hong Kong, we've gone to Japan, we've gone to Paris. Florida... we're coming for you soon!

Wouldn't you love to have a brand that people thought about with such fondness?

That's the business obituary for Disney according to Chris Ducker.

What I'm getting at here is that you want your business to be remembered. My family will remember Disney parks as giving us the best of times. (And yes, we're big fans of the movies and all the rest of Disney, too.) Talk about legacy—that's legacy right there. Our trips there are experiences we will value forever. A business like Disney creates millions and millions of stories just like ours, stories of how the company changed lives. My Disney story is an example of exactly how important it is to affect lives.

Write your business obituary, and start to envision the kind of impact you can have on people simply because they experienced what you have to offer.

At the end of the day, we're talking about defining who you are here.

Your brand is what people say about you when you are at that dinner party, industry conference, coffee meeting, or networking event.

That's why you've got to do things right at the beginning of this entire process and define what you are all about, what you want to be known for, and how you want to be remembered. It is what people say about you when you're not around that counts. That's your brand, and that's why it's so darn important.

2

DEFINING YOUR PERFECT CUSTOMER

KNOWING who you are and what you are all about is just the beginning. From there, truly successful Youpreneurs get to work on defining and knowing their perfect customer. Defining your perfect customer is just as important as defining who you are.

If you think about it logically, you can't sell to someone you don't know. I've been lucky to have been trained in the sales industry from a very young age. I was 17 when I got my first part-time sales job. I have sold pretty much everything to anyone you can think of. I used to sell second-hand cars. I couldn't even drive a car at the time, nor did I have an inkling as to what was going on underneath the hood. Fortunately for me, sales comes down to knowing your customer.

One day a young lady walked onto the car lot I was working at. She was perhaps 20 years old and with her mother. After just a few minutes of rapport building, it was clear that she was looking forward to the independence of having her own car and "going out with the girls." I jumped into action, pointing out the fact that it was a five-seater, had lots of room for her friends, and that the boot (or trunk, for my American friends!) had plenty of space for shopping bags!

We went for a spin and enjoyed a couple of tunes on the radio on our way back to the showroom—I even sang along to one of them with her! I sold the car, even though it was over their budget, by highlighting what I knew about the customer: she wanted room for her friends, her shopping bags, and a great stereo to play their favorite tunes on as they hung out together.

If you can define your perfect customer as early on as possible, you're going to be off to the races rather than plodding along trying to figure it all out as you go.

Building Your Customer Avatar

The easiest way to identify your perfect customer is to build what's called your "customer avatar." I am about as serious as I can get about developing an avatar and doing it early on. You'll need to switch off a little from defining what you have to offer and start asking yourself some clear questions about the type of people you want to serve.

You've got to understand what their story is, and you want that story to be as detailed as possible.

- What's their background?
- What are they up to right now?
- What situations are they currently in?
- How old are they?
- Where do they live?
- Are they married or are they single?

- Do they have kids?
- What are they struggling with right now?

By giving your avatar this depth of background and placing them in a real-world scenario, you essentially are building out their lives.

Defining your customers enables you not just to sell to them properly, but also to figure out what and why they're going to buy.

It's important to understand what your customers want, or you end up blindly pitching somebody something. That's not the best way to make sales. If you've established the "know, love, and trust" that I spoke of earlier, then you should have built rapport with your customers and solidified their trust in you. Now it's time to actually understand what they want so you can create the perfect product or service for them.

Every little detail that you can come up with will get you one step closer to figuring out exactly what you will need to do in order to convert your perfect prospect into your best customer. Developing their story is very important, and you want to be as thorough as possible. Here are a few more areas to think about:

- What age group are they in: Baby Boomers? Millennials?
- How much money do they make every year?
- What's their disposable income?

And here's a tip: assigning an age group has to be much more than just saying, *Mary is between 30 and 45 years old.* That statement doesn't really mean a whole lot with no other context around it. Instead, give Mary a life consistent with her age: *Mary is 41 years old, and a member of Generation Y. She has been married for 13 years, and she and her husband have two sons, ages 10 and 12. The family just relocated to a mid-size city for her job, and she got a moderate raise to do so. She now makes $83,000 per*

Defining your customers enables you not just to **sell to them properly**, but also to figure out **what and why they're going to buy**.

year, and she is looking forward to having more money this year to put toward her family's second trip to Hawaii and maybe even a business-building conference happening locally. Last year, Mary completed an online coaching certification course, and she is currently doing free consulting in the early mornings and on weekends to get experience and exposure.

Understanding the Importance of Customer Motivations

Once you start diving a little deeper into Mary's life, you understand what she is all about. You get to know what her motivations are. You understand her struggles a little bit more. Different people struggle with different things at different points in their lives, right? Not only that—people have different levels of income and savings at different times in their lives.

Somebody in their 40s, for example, has probably been through a few ups and downs and has probably learned some pretty costly lessons. This person is usually a little bit more cash flush. They might have some savings. They might understand exactly what their disposable income is every month. They might go on holiday on a regular basis. What motivates them to take that break? All these little different details about them are very, very important.

Now, someone in their 30s may not be at the point yet where they have extra money to invest in what you have to offer. They are more likely to be in the early stages of building their family, which consumes a great deal of their money and time, making it harder for them to buy what you're selling.

People over 65 may have more free money than either of the two age groups discussed so far, but then again, seniors may be on more of a fixed income, causing them to have less free money to play with. So it's very important to understand what the age group of your perfect customer will be, and to know what motivates people at certain times in their lives.

Once you understand what your customers are struggling with, you can then start providing solutions to those problems. This is at the very core of being an entrepreneur: you're a problem solver. The more you know about your customers' situations, their problems really, the better.

You need to know where people are in life, just as much as you need to know who they are.

- Are they working full-time?
- Are they wanting to escape the nine-to-five rat race and become an entrepreneur?
- Have they developed a side hustle and come home from their nine-to-five job to work for two hours in the basement or in their spare bedroom on building their blog or teaching people how to be X, Y, Z?
- If they are working on the side, how long have they been doing that?
- Are they sick and tired of their job and want to break free and work on their side hustle 100 percent of the time?
- Does Monday morning come around, and they're dragging their feet to the office?
- Are they already a full-time entrepreneur? Do they already have their own business?
- Are they making money?
- Do they want to make more money?
- Are they in debt?
- What's their favorite color?*
    *No, I'm not kidding. Trust me, you want to get this detailed.

Knowing about all these circumstances enables you to understand who you're actually going to be talking to. Then, it all comes down to how you can help them.

By defining your perfect customer with this level of detail, you can get a pretty precise idea of where their pain points are. Understanding what they're struggling with will enable you to solve those problems.

If you solve people's problems well and if you do it in a trustworthy manner with a good price point attached to it, people will be happy to pay for the convenience of you helping them out based on your experience.

And here's the thing—once you understand who it is you're actually going to be helping, you'll get this innate ability to find them in the real world.

> To make this exercise super easy for you, I've created an in-depth Process Blueprint. You can download it instantly and for free at **Youpreneur** .com/ReadersOnly

Figuring Out How You Can Help Them

Now you have to go a little deeper. You now know what your avatar is struggling with, but what is holding that customer back from a solution? Let's use the example of somebody who's running a business and feeling absolutely overwhelmed by their workload. They're just trying to do too much all the time by themselves.

We know the solution to that problem is to hire people who can come in and help relieve some of that pressure. But what are the pain points that have led our business owner to do everything himself in the first place?

Well, number one, the owner could be the problem. Sometimes owners can't get over themselves and understand that there might be people out there who could do particular tasks better than they can. They just don't want to admit it. So that could be a possible pain point. Another might be that our owner has had a bad experience in the past hiring people. The owner maybe hired the wrong people, they didn't work out, and the whole process wasted time and money.

Once you identify the pain points, you can address the overall struggle that your customer is experiencing and present solutions.

Now, there are two ways that you can present those solutions to your customer. You can offer them for a fee, or you can offer them for free. Actually, both ways are valid and very much aligned with each other, particularly when building The Business of You. My only caution about free versus paid is that you don't want to be the freebie person in your industry. I'll talk about monetization later on in the book, but I want to just touch on this right now.

You must be seen to sell in order to build influence.

There's a fine balance that must be maintained between what information you are giving away for free and the rest of the information that you charge a fee for.

You can help people by answering some questions relating to their pain points and their struggles for free, but you don't want to give the entire house away. Let's revisit the example of somebody struggling with hiring a team. Let's say you can give business owners three examples of great questions to ask on every interview to make sure they hire the right person. You could write a blog post or create a podcast episode that will explain how to handle the interview process and include the three questions you want to share. You can offer that much information for free, but when business owners interview these people, you know they are going to ask more than three questions, right? There may be seven or eight more questions you can offer to them to make each interview the best process possible for finding the right help. Those seven or eight questions could be delivered in a product you charge for. That's your entry-level product for helping somebody struggling with solving their team-building issue.

My point is, you want to give away as much as you possibly can, but not the whole farm.

It's the difference between helping people for nothing and helping in a way that also builds your influence and your reach. You can use blog posts, podcasts, videos, and social media to give away good, sound, free information that leads your audience to recognize that you are the expert they need to work with. But you're not giving away all your information. You want to hold some back so that you can ultimately monetize what you know in order to grow your business.

Think about the problems and pain points that your avatar is experiencing. Now start attaching ways you can help solve those problems, and you are on your way. Once you are rolling with this sort of mindset, building successful relationships with your real customers will be much easier.

You must **be seen to sell** in order to build influence.

Customer Wants, Versus What You Think They Want

At this point, you know who you are, and you now know who your perfect customer is as well. However, you haven't interacted with that perfect customer all that much. You might have talked to a few prospects and understood their particular situations—maybe you've done a few Skype calls or spoken with a few friends who you believe are probably close to your perfect avatar. At this point, all you can do is work out what you *think* they want and need. You haven't had enough interaction with them to actually *know*, so you have to guess at exactly what they are looking for.

You will find as time goes by that people will start to tell you what they want you to help them with, and then it's up to you to switch your approach. Instead of offering what you *think* customers want, you start to help them in ways that you now KNOW they actually *need*.

The importance of trust and rapport building can't be overstated. Once people trust you and they've learned a few useful things from you, they'll start to open up and share what they really need, and that's when the magic happens.

That's when you can start really building out your online home—the place where you'll create all this helpful content to spearhead the growth of your brand and business and become the go-to source in your industry.

3

BUILDING YOUR ONLINE HOME

TECHNOLOGY has changed the game. You no longer hang a shingle on the side of a building, say you're open for business, and wait for customers to wander in. The Internet has opened up so many opportunities to interact with the whole world—businesses are no longer restricted to a physical location.

But the question is, how do you build an online presence that truly captivates your audience? How do you establish an environment where people can get to know you, fall in love with you, and start to trust you?

Setting up your website properly is really the true start to building your online brand. Your website must have the look and feel of what you're all about. If it doesn't, you could create a disconnect between your message and your prospect or client. (See, there's a reason why becoming a Youpreneur is a process and why understanding who you are was the first step!)

Your website should reflect you. If you are super professional, then your online home must look super professional. That means professional fonts, professional colors, and a business-like layout. If, on the other hand, you're a little quirky and you want to be remembered for a particular trait that makes you stand out, then you should include that quirk in your look and feel. For example, if you're the guy who always wears orange-framed glasses, then you may want to have orange-framed glasses on the top of your website or in your logo. And you'll want to use the color orange throughout your branding.

When people discover your online home for the first time, do you want them to take a certain action? Maybe opt in to your email list or watch a video? Regardless of what you want your newly discovered prospect to do, it will be a cinch to direct them if the look and the feel of your website is spot-on.

Getting the Look and Feel Right

Let's break this down a little bit. The look and feel of your online home should reflect not only you, but also your business niche and your perfect customer. For example, if you're a life coach, you might want to consider using earth-toned colors and script-styled fonts—specific touches that communicate the success and achievement your clients can expect from working with you. The site's icons and images should be consistent with your business market as well. Everything on your site should appeal directly to your perfect customer.

If you sell scuba-diving excursions, using greens and blues on your website will show people that your business is all about getting them in the ocean. Images of fish or coral will project what your customers expect to see when using your products or services.

Let's say your audience is driven, ambitious entrepreneurs. To communicate market domination and achievement, you will likely want to use bold colors and strong, heavy, dense fonts. Dark reds and blues are pretty popular here (think Gary Vaynerchuk), but brighter colors aren't out of the question either—just look at millionaire online business owner Ramit Sethi, whose online home is full of bright yellows, cool greys, and shades of green.

Aren't you glad I made you think about your perfect customer's favorite color in the last chapter? This is why.

You have to understand your audience—who it is you're going after. Certain colors and fonts are known to do better in particular markets, and knowing which ones will work best to attract your perfect customer is going to be crucial to the success of your look and feel.

The one style rule I am absolute about is that fonts must be readable. It never ceases to amaze me when I go to someone's website and they have used fonts that are not legible. What a disaster.

You have six seconds to grab somebody's attention when they come to your website the first time, and you need to make each one of those seconds count!

If you lose a prospect in those first six seconds, or if they can't figure out who you are, what you do, and why they should spend more time with you, you're going to lose them forever. The fact is, you never get a second chance to make a great first impression.

We've talked color and font and imagery, the look and feel of the site, but another important element of that first impression of your online home is your tagline. Your tagline is what confirms to the visitor that they are in the right place.

You've probably heard of the elevator pitch, right? If you meet somebody in an elevator, you've got about 15 to 20 seconds

You have **six seconds to grab somebody's attention** when they come to your website the first time, and you need to make each one of those seconds count!

to tell them exactly what you do to spark some level of interest so you can potentially end up doing business with them in the future.

Your website needs an elevator pitch. However, you don't want someone to have to read an entire paragraph to understand exactly what you are all about. That's where your tagline comes into play.

Your tagline should answer the question, "What do you do?" But that answer must be benefit driven. Let's take my business, for example, and answer the question, "What does Chris Ducker do?" My tagline is

I help people become the go-to source in their industry and build a successful business around their expertise!

Maybe you're a professional dog walker. Your tagline could be, *I help keep your dog fit and healthy while you get on with your life*. Whatever your business, your tagline is critical. People should spend a lot more time crafting it than they usually do. To understand what your tagline should be, you have to know what your audience needs, wants, or could benefit from. A perfect tagline means you have defined your business and your customer.

The easiest way to do this is to talk to as many people as possible who are in line with your perfect customer avatar. Communication is the key to any good, solid relationship.

Listening to your market will almost always produce the best and correct answers.

However, communicating with your audience could prove more difficult than you imagine, ironically, because there are so many options. This is actually a genuine problem. With all the choices, the conversation has become quite fragmented.

Take the blogging world, for example. When blogging started, you would create content and post it to your blog. Then your audience would read that blog post and have the opportunity to leave comments, and that would be where you would spend the majority of the time interacting with your audience.

Nowadays the bulk of the conversation and interaction with your audience will likely take place on some sort of social media platform. It has been made so clear to me that this is true that I went as far as turning comments off on my blog a few years ago because I found that I was getting more interaction on my social media channels in regards to my online content than I was on the platform that the content was actually living on.

Getting Started with Online Content

Starting out as a Youpreneur, you want to communicate with your consumers as much as you can. Your goal is to grab and hold your audience's attention as long as possible, and to do that you need to figure out how to bring them into a conversation that allows you to help them solve their problems or fill their needs. Sounds like a tall order? The key is to create content that compels site visitors to go deeper into what you are offering. One of the best ways to do that is to try and have every single piece of content you create do one of the following:

1. Entertain
2. Educate
3. Inspire

Every single piece of online content, whether it be a blog post, a podcast, a video, an infographic, an image for social media, a quote on Twitter—it doesn't matter what it is—every single piece should do one of those three things.

From time to time, you might actually be able to amalgamate all three qualities in a single piece of content, and that's what I call just plain showing off! That's overachiever-type stuff right there. But seriously, before going live with any piece of content, you always want to ask if it entertains, educates, or inspires your audience.

The Searchable Power of Written Blog Posts

What's the first thing you do when you want to know the answer to a question? Smart money says you go online, probably to Google, and type in whatever topic you need to know about. Then Google, in its infinite wisdom, will produce a series of results for you, all clickable. The majority of those links will take you to written content. Now here's your mission: when your perfect customers go searching, you want as many of those clickable links as possible to point to your website.

Listening to **your market** will almost always produce the **best and correct answers.**

All great online homes start with highly valuable blog content, which is searchable by Google and the other search engine powers that be. And all great blog content begins with a great title. Titles are what start off a conversation, and to get started on the right foot, you want to pay attention to how you get the readers' attention in the first place. Here's an example of a title that has done very well for me in the past.

Passion versus Profit: Which One
Will Build a Stronger Business?

What I'm doing here is prefacing my blog with a time-honored conversation starter—"Which is better?" And note that it has value for my audience: Should I build a business based purely on passion or on profit? Which one is going to help me build a stronger business?

Here's another one:

If Business Isn't Converting, You Need This Solution!

You see what I'm doing? I'm highlighting a problem and saying, "You need to click here to find out what the solution to that problem is."

Another one that went viral for me was

Five New Words for Entrepreneurial Fear

What am I doing here? I'm pressing the emotional button. We all fear something at some point, and I'm challenging people to look at fear in different ways. I want the reader to think, "If I'm not going to call it fear anymore, what should I be calling it? Well, Chris has given me five new words. That's great. Let's look at those."

I think probably one of the most popular posts I've done in the last couple of years was

The Power and Duty of Entrepreneurial Professionalism

I talked a little while ago about how the entry barrier is at an all-time low to calling yourself an entrepreneur, and in that post I really broke the problem down and described it in full detail. That piece struck a number of different nerves for a lot of people, and it was shared like crazy all over the Internet.

So as you start building out your content, you really need to focus in on both attention-grabbing titles and benefit-driven titles. Whichever tack you take, a title should let people know exactly what they're going to be getting when they click on your link to read your content.

Keyword-rich titles will help people connect with your content and make them want to read further, but they also help people discover your content in the first place. The best content in the world does no one any good if it can't be found easily.

The two words people type in most often when they go to the Google search bar are *how to*. People are usually looking for information on a certain problem that they want to solve. For me, without a doubt, the best type of content to create, particularly when you're starting out, is *how to* content.

"How to Promote Facebook Live Videos," or "How to Create an Online Content Calendar," or "How to Become a Professional Speaker," or "How to Train Your Dog." Whatever solution people are looking for, it almost always starts with "how to."

Think about the question you are looking to answer.

Titles are a very important part to any successful content, but a close second would be what I like to call *scanner subtitles*. People are scanners. No one has the time to sit and read a 1,000-word blog post anymore. The time we have for any activity has diminished horribly over the last couple of decades. What do you do before you buy a book in a bookstore? You open it up, scan it, and then decide whether you want to buy it or not. You might have done it with this book, or if you purchased it online, you probably read the table of contents or some of the reader reviews.

The strategy here is to break your blog text into sections using subtitles that will jump out at the readers. Making your content scannable will satisfy the modern audience's appetite for short, easily consumable bits of content.

You've got to preload your site with a fair amount of content. Your blog is just one part of your website. When you first start out, you don't want to have a website that only has one or two blog posts on it. You might have a podcast, you might have a video archive, and you definitely should have an About page. I'd say a good number to shoot for would be 10 pieces of content that you know are going to help solve individual problems for the people who will discover you.

Why Consistency Is Your Website's Best Friend

Once you get going and you've got those 10 pieces of content up on your site, you can't just walk away and leave it like that. The search engines will fall in love with a website, meaning they will serve up that link in their results, if it *A) has lots of helpful, original content on it,* and *B) has new high-value content added to it on a regular and consistent basis.*

Consistency is the single most important thing here. It's even more important to be consistent than it is to be concerned with volume. Being consistent by blogging on Wednesday every single week for weeks on end will get you more Google love than blogging one week on Tuesday, then next Friday, then the next week on Saturday. You've got to be consistent. It's not just important for the Google love you'll get, but also for the love of your audience.

With every piece of content you create, every interaction you have with your audience, the goal is to become somebody's favorite. The way you do that is by being consistent, serving your audience on a regular basis, and being reliable.

The **best content** you can create is **content that promotes other content**.

Think about your favorite TV show. Before Netflix, which has allowed us to become binge watchers, your favorite show would go live at the same time on the same day every week, and you would tune in to watch it. You'd look forward to that particular show in that particular time slot. You'd mark it on your calendar so you wouldn't miss it. There's no time for the gym on Thursday night because *CSI* is on at 9:00 p.m.! You know what I mean? It's more important to be consistent in putting out content than to be prolific. It's not about sheer volume.

Ultimately, adding new content a couple of times a week is good. I remember when I first started blogging back in January 2010, I was blogging on Monday, Wednesday, and Friday. I committed to doing that for a year, but truth be told, in the last

However, it's not just having people consume your content; you **want them to share your content, too!**

few months of that year, I couldn't wait to go down to once or twice a week. I will say this, though: by the time that year was up, I had a ton of content that I'd created, and it was much easier for me to then build on that archive going forward.

The best content you can create is content that promotes other content.

Here's a little ninja tip: create links in your newer blog content to help promote your older content.

Remember all the stuff that you published a month ago, six months ago, a year ago? You should also link from that to more recent content. This is something that hardly anybody does, and it will serve you well. If you're creating the type of "evergreen" content that's going to help people solve problems, then it will be valuable long after you initially publish it.

These days, I create three pieces of content on a regular basis, but they are not all blog posts. I blog once a week on Monday, I add video to my YouTube channel every Wednesday (which is also embedded on my blog), and I publish an episode of the *Youpreneur FM* podcast once a week, every Friday. We'll talk more on video and podcast content in the next section of the book.

To help you not only create great blog content, but also get a jump on marketing those blog posts when they go live (we'll be deep-diving much further into the marketing side of things later on!), here's my step-by-step roadmap on how to create and promote a blog post successfully.

HOW TO CREATE & PROMOTE A BLOG POST

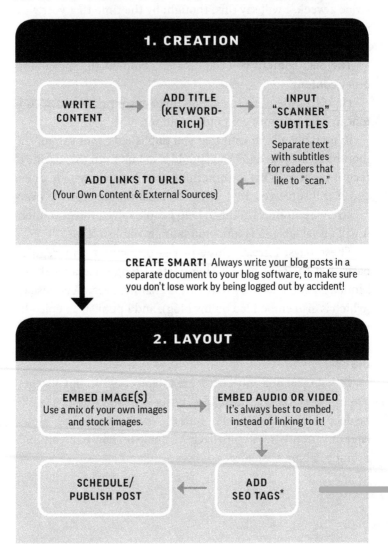

1. CREATION

WRITE CONTENT → **ADD TITLE (KEYWORD-RICH)** → **INPUT "SCANNER" SUBTITLES**

Separate text with subtitles for readers that like to "scan."

ADD LINKS TO URLS (Your Own Content & External Sources) ←

CREATE SMART! Always write your blog posts in a separate document to your blog software, to make sure you don't lose work by being logged out by accident!

2. LAYOUT

EMBED IMAGE(S) Use a mix of your own images and stock images. → **EMBED AUDIO OR VIDEO** It's always best to embed, instead of linking to it!

SCHEDULE/ PUBLISH POST ← **ADD SEO TAGS***

*SEO TAGGING

One of the biggest mistakes bloggers make is not including the correct SEO tags on their blog posts. They are as follows:

→ Post Title
→ Meta Description
→ Keywords
→ Alt Tag on Image

3. PROMOTION

PUBLISH THE BLOG POST → **ALERT YOUR EMAIL SUBSCRIBERS OF THE NEW CONTENT**

↓

"NEXT LEVEL" MARKETING! ← **POST LINKS AND IMAGES TO SOCIAL MEDIA**
If promoting via Twitter, tweet link every 6 hours for 48 hours.

"NEXT LEVEL" MARKETING: Go Beyond Email & Social Media
Going the extra mile can make a huge difference to eyeballs on your new post.
Think of live video broadcasts, discussing the post content, short video trailers,
and Twitter chats to create buzz and conversation.

4. MARKETING

SCHEDULE SOCIAL MEDIA
Use social media software to schedule mentions regularly—
keep your archive alive!

LINK TO/FROM FRESH CONTENT
Keep new content fresh by linking to your archive.

MENTION IN PODCASTS/VIDEOS
Casually drop in mentions (and links) when suitable.

INSERT INTO YOUR EMAIL AUTO-RESPONDER
Not all your posts, but the important, high-value ones!

Communicating with your audience through your website is crucial, and you want to ensure that what you are posting is strong enough to keep people coming back for more. This is true of any content you create and is not limited to just your written blog posts. Whether you create a great blog post, video, social media post, or podcast episode, it all comes down to understanding your customer and understanding the best way to communicate with that person you want consuming the content.

However, it's not just having people consume your content; you want them to share your content, too!

That's how you get that ripple effect, and then suddenly you're enjoying the viral action of people sharing and spreading what you're all about.

Setting Up Your Email Marketing

Getting people to your website and providing them with enough content to pique their interest is step one in the process of attracting prospects and converting those prospects to clients.

Step two is building an email list and communicating with the folks on that list in a helpful, strategic, and consistent (that word again!) fashion. Almost every expert will tell you that the most important part of your online business is your email list. Many entrepreneurs have gone through sort of a love-hate relationship with email marketing. For me personally, it's still the most important thing in my business. Even now with Facebook ads being as targeted as they are and being as affordable as they are, email is still the primary way for me to communicate with my audience.

The funny thing is that if you work with any Facebook ad manager, they will all ask you for your email list so they can

Solve somebody's problem, properly and in a quick manner... you'll gain an instant fan!

retarget your email list subscribers on Facebook via advertisements. So, even if Facebook advertising is your goal, you want to start building your list as early as possible.

The Power of the "Quick Win" Opt-In

A little earlier on, I mentioned opt-ins, or getting your audience members to opt in to your list. An opt-in magnet, if you're not familiar with this term, is the thing you dangle in front of a prospect to entice them to sign up to your email list. Ultimately, that requires them to give up their email address in exchange for whatever it is you are offering. That opt-in magnet should be a piece of content that will help them solve a problem. You want to offer them a quick win.

Think about the avatar you created for your perfect client and the struggles they are experiencing. Find the pain points connected with those struggles and figure out the one pain point that you can solve for somebody in a very quick way.

That should be your opt-in magnet.

Make sure your opt-in is not just some fluffy piece of content or some lousy looking e-book that you just slapped together. I always say that your opt-in magnet should be something that you could easily put a price tag on of at least $100.

Solve somebody's problem, properly and in a quick manner... you'll gain an instant fan!

By giving your prospects that quick win, they're more likely not only to stay on your email list, but also to talk about you, spread what you're all about, and then further down the line buy something you've created to solve a bigger problem for them. That's what an opt-in magnet does.

Let's say, for example, you are somebody who teaches how to produce great online videos. One of your opt-in magnets could be a *10-Step Checklist to Get Your YouTube Channel Looking Great,* or perhaps you offer the guide to the *Five Pieces You Must Have to Shoot Great Online Videos on a Budget.* Those will give your prospects information they can use and give them what they need to get a quick win.

Getting that quick win is important, but you want to try to make your magnet part of what I call your "value ladder" too.

You're solving a problem with a quick win, but how does that quick win open up the doors for bigger wins for them further down the line? And bigger purchases for you as the product or service creator?

Let's return to the example of the business owner who teaches people how to produce online videos. The quick wins created as opt-in magnets will give prospects the basics they need to get started. Further down the line, the site owner might create a short online video course, which could give one to three hours' worth of content that sells for $97 to $497. That course could teach people not only how to further use and extend what they learned in the opt-in offer, but also how to create a great final piece of video content that will ultimately allow them to be able to market their business in an effective way—thus producing ongoing leads and additional business for them.

We'll go much further into the subject of monetization later on, but do you see how it works?

It's not just about creating a quick win for the sake of getting people to opt in; it's also thinking further down the line as to how you are going to help people above and beyond that quick win. More importantly, it's about how you are going to convince them to actually engage in a monetary transaction with you next time, and then have them become a long-term paying customer.

Don't Just Deliver, Overdeliver—Early On!

Getting the opt-in magnet you've promised to your new email subscriber is just the beginning. Sure, they signed up for the magnet—or, more specifically, the solution it'll give them—but you don't want to just send that one email and forget about them. You want to bring people back to the site and further the value you are offering them. You have more solutions for their problems. How will you let them know?

You should seriously consider setting up an email autoresponder funnel that'll automatically send those newly signed-up customers another batch of emails with more content and more value to serve them. Sure, it's a bit of work upfront, but the payoff could be huge in winning a fan for life.

INTRO EMAIL FUNNEL

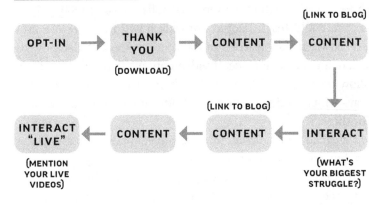

For a complete list of all the services and software that I personally use to execute everything I've discussed in this chapter and throughout the rest of the book, visit **Youpreneur.com/ReadersOnly**

Overall, people tend to over-think email funnels. I like to keep things really, really simple. Here's a sample introduction funnel that you can use that'll deliver on your promise, and then overdeliver, to win 'em over for good!

Now you are on your way. You have designed a website with the right look and feel, put together content that captivates your audience through a blog and other publishing media, created an amazing opt-in magnet, and followed up with your email list, letting customers know about products that can offer them even more value. These are the essentials for building an online presence that really captivates your audience and creates an environment where people can get to know you, fall in love with you, and learn to trust you.

CASE STUDY

NAME: Roger Edwards
BUSINESS NAME: Roger Edwards Marketing
WEBSITE: RogerEdwards.co.uk

Background

Roger Edwards had clocked 25 years in marketing roles in UK financial services and had worked his way up to marketing direc-tor of several big brands. Complexity, in all parts of the marketing mix, frustrated Roger. Strategy was tedious and demotivating and yet so important to the success of any business. Throughout his career he had been a leader pushing simplicity. Roger knew he could make strategy easier.

Understanding the massive potential, Roger launched a blog for one brand but had to keep it out of the IT estate, almost a secret, to get it out there. It seemed he was the only one who wanted to experiment with content marketing. Roger decided he wanted to leave big corporate, set himself up as a consultant, and help people who were excited about digital and social and wanted to keep their marketing strategy simple.

Establishing Authority

On leaving big corporate, Roger had the advantage of a strong media profile in the financial services industry. People knew who he was and recognized him as a good communicator, a motivating speaker, and someone always going on about cutting complexity and bloat.

Keeping his name out there was Roger's first goal. He launched the *Marketing and Finance Podcast* in June 2014 and used social media, his existing network, and a slowly growing email list to promote it. Roger knew this was a long game, and he had to be consistent. Few people in the UK professional services even knew what a podcast was then.

Over the first six months doubt did creep in. Roger's profile was still high, but the business was not coming his way. Then he published episode 33 of his podcast and got some work from a listener. Show number 96 netted a five-figure project. Consistency pays off!

In order to keep his authority intact, he continued to write media articles, accept the odd free speaking gig, and experiment with new social media to push his message and engage with customers.

Roger refined the focus of the message over time. Starting with loads of offers, writing, training, strategy development, and content creation, Roger started to hone in on "simple strategy" as his core service. Weaving this message into his content helped move his personal brand from "FS marketing guy" to "keep marketing simple guy."

Three Things to Grow Business Effectively

1. The podcast continues to be the foundation of Roger's content strategy. The show brings in a steady stream of inquiries that lead to proposals that lead to contracts. Roger complements the podcast with pre-recorded marketing tips videos, behind the scenes RogVLOGs, and Facebook Live broadcasts, all focusing on the simple strategy message.

2. Roger has worked hard to turn simple strategy into a genuine model from which he can write a book, develop courses, create more video, and give the podcast an even stronger core theme. Roger realized that in all those corporate years of enduring endless strategy workshops, SWOT analysis, PEST analysis, and

the four and seven "Ps" of marketing, he'd created a framework in his mind which he used but had never written down. Now, Roger has developed, through several Youpreneur mastermind sessions, his "Goal—Offer—Activity" model.

3. In Roger's corporate career, he was a prolific speaker, from small workshops to giant events, both UK conferences and international. In the first few years of building his business, Roger did accept a few speaking opportunities, but it wasn't a priority. Now that Roger has a clearer focus and has developed his "simple strategy" theme into a model, he has started to seek out speaking engagements again.

Most Profitable Monetization

Roger's one-day workshop based around the "Goal—Offer—Activity" model is his most profitable offering. When he ran the session for a big corporation for the first time, he expected much resistance due to their reliance on established, complex, and intellectual models. But they gave him amazing feedback.

Here's what Roger had to say about being a YOUPRENEUR:

Working on your own is lonely. The one thing I missed about corporate life was instant access to peers to bounce around ideas, receive encouragement, and be held accountable. The Youpreneur Community has filled that gap for me. Peers in corporates can also be negative and demotivating or have their own political agenda. Not so in Youpreneur—with the lack of ego, it is a strong incubator for great ideas.

The masterminds I've attended have helped narrow my focus and develop the model upon which my business will grow in the future.

4

SETTING UP YOUR SOCIAL MEDIA

L ET'S face it. Gone are the days of keeping your business life and your personal life separate. With the introduction of the various social media platforms, we all find our social and professional lives intertwining. At the same time, we are trying to maintain a professional relationship with our audience. It's a balance, for sure.

So the question is, *Is there a way, in a constructive manner that won't drive us nuts, to truly integrate the power of being social online with our business?*

The short answer is, *Of course there is,* but I want to preface this answer with a very important public service announcement. I see way too many people actually building their entire businesses on social media platforms. This is a recipe for disaster.

Let's say you've built a great community with a Facebook group, for example. You've got 20,000 or 30,000 people in the group, and there's lots of communication going on. You're using that group to pitch your products and your services—and it works. People buy from you. Everything is rolling along nicely. However, at the same time, you're so focused on the group (on Mr. Zuckerberg's platform) that you're not at all focused on getting those people off of Facebook and over to your online home (your website) and your email subscriber list.

If you are not focusing on getting your community off of Facebook (or Twitter, Instagram, YouTube, LinkedIn, or anywhere else online that you have no real control over) and into your own privately owned ecosystem, then you are fundamentally building your home on rented land.

Sooner or later, it is going to come to bite you in the you-know-where. It's not a matter of *if*, it's just a matter of *when*. So I'll say it very clearly...

Don't build your online home on rented land.

Instead, use social media to expand on communication and to enhance relationships that you build with your customers. It shouldn't be the primary source of anything and everything with your audience. It should be an additional venue for communication. I want that to be very clear as we continue to move forward.

Don't build **your online home** on **rented land**.

Social media can, could, and should become part of building your online community. People are social beings, and we want to be in communication with other people. Companies like Facebook, Twitter, LinkedIn, and Instagram make it very easy for us to communicate with each other whether we are sitting at a laptop or a desktop computer or, most likely nowadays, on our mobile devices. In today's marketplace, you can't ignore social media any longer, and you should incorporate some aspect of social interaction in your business, but don't let it become the primary focus.

So, let's spend some time looking at how to do this right.

How Images Can Make or Break Your Social Profiles

When setting up your social profiles, there are a few things you should keep in mind. These, actually, come down to common sense. The first item is the look and feel of the images you use on social media platforms.

Your Main Profile Image

You are on a Youpreneur journey to become the go-to source in your industry. Because you are your brand, reaching that goal becomes a lot easier if people see the same image of you everywhere. It's like McDonald's. You don't even need to see the name—just show us the golden arches and we know it's a McDonald's restaurant.

I admit it drives me nuts and is a real pet peeve of mine when I see people using different profile photos from one platform to another. Using different photos isn't going to be the end of your business, but it isn't helping it either, and I wish people would stop doing it.

For example, on Twitter someone may use a picture of himself sitting in a shirt, jacket, and tie. On Facebook, they'll have a recent picture with a birthday cake next to their head. On Instagram, they'll have a picture holding up their kids. Don't do this. It's confusing. If you're looking to build your business based on you, your brand, and your experience, you've got to have the same photo, or headshot, on all of your platforms.

There is one exception to this rule, and that is your cover image. Almost all of those networks I just mentioned—Twitter, Facebook, LinkedIn (the exception is Instagram)—allow you to have a cover image of some kind.

Getting Creative with Your Cover Image

The cover image is a larger image that allows you to showcase what you're all about, visually. It's an image you should change on a regular basis. You can use it to

- Promote your products when you're launching them.
- Promote an event you might be speaking at.
- Promote an event that you're holding that you want to sell tickets for.

Actually, you can use it to promote anything at all. Maybe it's the second anniversary of your bestselling book. Whatever the case may be, you can use your cover image on a regular basis to get people to take action based on an offer you're making.

You have to always be mindful that you are using social media to market your business. I have seen a lot of business owners and entrepreneurs get into trouble when they forget this and blend their personal and business communication a bit too much.

As a Youpreneur, you are your brand. Anything you say, share, or do will help your audience to build their own perception of you!

Bestselling author Hal Elrod uses his cover image space to promote his book to his followers, with a clear call to action to buy it.

Online business mentor Amy Porterfield uses her cover image to simply, yet very efficiently, tell her audience how she can help them.

I use the cover image real estate on my Facebook profile to promote our annual event in London, with a clear call to action to grab a ticket!

As we already know, their perception will become your reality. Your audience will ultimately end up shaping the way your business pivots and grows over the years. We've got to respect that fact from the outset and understand that we are 100 percent in control of the way our audience thinks about us when we're not around.

Here are a few guidelines for images on social media:

- Only use high-quality images.
- Only use up-to-date images.
- Always use the same profile image across all platforms.

As a Youpreneur, **you are your brand**. Anything you say, share, or do will help your audience to build their own perception of you!

A Few Notes on Social Bios

Your social bio is second only to imagery in its importance on social media. And just like your images, your bio should remain identical, or as close to it as possible, across all platforms. Some important guidelines to follow when creating your social bio are

- Mention how you can help anyone checking out your profile.
- Keep it brief—less than 100 words is best, if not half that.
- Sing your own praises, but don't go overboard.
- Keep it focused on the solutions you provide to your customer's problems.
- Answer the question "What's in it for me?" for the visitor.

As an example, here's a snapshot of my Twitter bio:

Chris Ducker ✔

@ChrisDucker

Helping YOU become the go-to expert in your market via my blog, podcast, online community and live events! Proud 🏴󠁧󠁢󠁥󠁮󠁧󠁿

⊙ Youpreneur HQ   🔗 chrisducker.com

737 Following   **67.7K** Followers

Using Social Video to Create Reactions

Social media posts and images are both effective ways to engage your audience, but there is another format that is sweeping in and taking the Internet world by storm—video.

I want to be very clear here: I do not think that everyone should do video!

Video content is a great way to get a message out, but not everyone is comfortable doing video, and that's okay. You have to decide for yourself if using video is right for you and your brand or not. I also don't want any Youpreneur creating content just because someone else told them they needed to.

There's a limit to any kind of content you create. If you start producing content just for the sake of producing it, you will end up putting out fluff.

With that said, I do believe that, if you can, you should absolutely use video in your online marketing. There are two types of video content that I want to touch on here.

There's **online video**, which is the kind of content I would put up on YouTube. This type of video should be properly edited, more planned out, and more educational in nature.

Don't forget, YouTube is owned by Google. It is the second-largest search engine on the Internet. The reason why that's so important is because when you're searching on Google, you will instantly get video links popping up in the results along with website links. Those videos are all from YouTube.

Here are a couple examples of my own YouTube video content:

ChrisDucker.com/How-To-Become-An-Influencer
(5 minutes, embedded from YouTube)

ChrisDucker.com/Brainstorm-Blog-Ideas
(7 minutes, embedded from YouTube)

Then there's what I call **social video**. This would be less produced and, nine times out of 10, live. This type of video could be used to engage an audience or offer more direct communication on a regular basis. I like to use social video to show "behind the scenes" of what I'm working on.

If I'm traveling to keynote a conference, for example, I might hop on Instagram Stories or go live on Periscope (Twitter's live video app) to talk about the event and what I'll be presenting on. Before I go on stage, I'll give my phone to somebody who happens to be there and have them either shoot a few clips of me on stage to upload later or even start a Facebook Live video on my official page and stream the entire keynote.

Just recently, I got bumped from business class to first class on a long-haul flight, so I put up a few videos of me in first class and showed everybody what it's like to live on the other side of big paychecks. My audience really likes that kind of stuff.

For an example of me using live social video to engage with my audience, check out this clip on my Facebook page:

ChrisDucker.com/FBLive-Email-Growth
(6 minutes, via Facebook Live)—a collection of short tips given to a live audience on growing an email list quickly and easily.

Human beings are naturally inquisitive. We're quite voyeuristic, if you think about it. Being able to use social video to show the behind the scenes of what you're all about is really fun, and it's an effective way to engage your audience in a new way and gain a deeper level of respect and trust.

I shared a video not so long ago of me backstage at an event. Just before I was introduced to the crowd, my wife was recording with my phone and sharing it to Instagram Stories (they disappear after 24 hours, much like Snapchat). She caught me getting mic'd up and shadowboxing and playing around with the camera.

The host of the event says, *Ladies and gentlemen, welcome to the stage, Chris Ducker!* With my wife still posting live video, I went running up the stairs and then walked out on stage to begin my closing keynote for the event. There was this one clip where the lights created a cool shadow and glow around me as I started to engage with the crowd. People eat that stuff up. They really love it!

I came offstage to a load of messages about the "pregame" stories that I had posted. It was great.

Use video in your social media strategy because of the way your audience reacts to it, not just for the sake of doing it!

And remember what I said earlier about the importance of consistency in your blogging and content creation—that travels over to social media too. Being consistent not only with the volume and the style of the social content you create, but with the look and feel of it as well, will make your social media access points the most effective they can be.

It's just like using the same profile photo on all of your platforms. You want each platform to look and feel as though it's an extension of your brand—because it is!

However, with all the different social platforms that exist, the secret to doing this successfully is to be very careful that you don't overextend yourself.

To Tweet, or Not to Tweet?

I suggest that you pick no more than three social media platforms you feel are going to serve you and your audience best. For me, that is Twitter, Facebook, and Instagram. I use each of those platforms for very different reasons.

On Twitter, what I like to do is interact directly with the people who retweet or comment on my content. The reason why I prefer Twitter to do that is that it's quick and easy—140

Use video in your social media strategy because of the way **your audience reacts to it**, not just for the sake of doing it!

characters. Everyone can afford a quick read of 140 characters, whether they're lining up for their green smoothie in the morning or they're in the back of an Uber on the way to the airport. Wherever the audience is and whatever they may be doing, they can always spare enough time for Twitter.

I also use Twitter to promote my archive of content. People will share things on Twitter a little more freely than they will on Facebook and Instagram because of the quick nature of its newsfeed—it's constantly updated several times a minute, so you'll be less intrusive if you post several times a day. That makes it a perfect avenue to get as much traction as possible for your content.

I use Facebook for more in-depth communication. I like to ask questions on Facebook when I want to get some feedback from my community. You can interact with your audience on a hot topic that you might be thinking about writing on or recording a podcast about. Sometimes, I use the platform to get personal—but still focus on feedback from the people who follow me. You're not limited to 140 characters so you can share a lot more information in each post or share a longer video. It's important to understand what you'll actually share on each platform you choose. Thinking this through will make it easier to incorporate different social media into your brand and get the most out of all of them.

The final platform, which I use on pretty much a daily basis, is Instagram. I like to share more behind the scenes stuff of what I'm all about on this platform. If you go to my Instagram page, you'll see pictures of me hanging out with my dog or playing basketball with my buddies, or see who I'm having an afternoon espresso with. It may sound weird that people would want to know what you're doing in the afternoon, but remember this is a social platform, and people like to feel connected to you in a personal way.

This is the way you'll build the following you need to build The Business of You.

No matter what the platform or content, always stay on brand, and whenever you get the opportunity to bring things back to your business, you should. Post by post, tweet by tweet, video by video, you're building an audience. Your own very special little tribe that wants to know what you're up to.

This gives you the perfect opportunity to talk about what you are working on any time you want. You might want to tell them about a book that you've just finished writing and discuss when you'll be launching it. Maybe you've just purchased a new gadget and you want to share your thoughts on it, because it's related to the work you do and the people you serve would benefit from using it too. You don't have to get spammy or sleazy, but whenever you get a chance to make a point and bring it back to your business and what you stand for as a Youpreneur, always make sure that you do it.

How Much Is Too Much and How Little Is Not Enough?

That's a question that could be asked about a lot of different topics, but when it comes to social media, I'm specifically talking about how much you actually post on which platform. There is no simple answer.

Test your audience and see how they react to the different types of social media posts you publish on a regular basis.

For example, like I mentioned, the timeline on Twitter moves very quickly. Because of that, you want to post often to Twitter to get in front of as much of your audience as possible. And try to automate as much of that action as you possibly can. I tweet six to eight times a day on my Twitter account, with automated tweets usually consisting of the title and maybe one

Test your audience and see how they react to the **different types of social media posts** you publish on a regular basis.

key takeaway of the archived content I'm promoting. I'll almost always include an image, too.

On Facebook, things move almost as quickly, but because of the way people turn on and off notifications, you probably don't want to be as active there as you would be on Twitter. You might want to only post a couple of times a day, but make those posts more in-depth. Allowing people time to respond and comment on your Facebook posts gives you the opportunity to interact with them directly. This can turn one post into an ongoing conversation with your audience, and that can be very powerful for your business.

As with Facebook, less may be more with Instagram as well. When you open up Instagram and you start flicking through your timeline, you don't want to see four or five images from the same person one after another, right? That's not the way to use it. I may only post to my Instagram profile once a day.

However, your Instagram Stories can be a very intimate connection with your audience members. I only get an average of 700 to 800 people watching my Instagram Stories (even though I have well over 25,000 followers on my main profile). But these followers are invested in the relationship they have with me. They're following the behind the scenes look into my life. They're seeing me in the back of an Uber, or with my wife on date nights, or with my youngest playing LEGO.

This is a more intimate connection, and I love it. In return, those followers love me. (Remember how important that is?!)

Overall, I believe you have to post what you need to say to your audience to get them to engage with you. If that means posting more or fewer times during the day, that is something you will need to gauge with your audience on each platform. You have to figure out where your sweet spot is going to be. Then be as consistent as possible based on your findings.

Is There a "Social Magic Hour"?

One question I get asked all the time in regards to posting to social media platforms is when is the best time to post, or is there a time you shouldn't post? It's pretty much open season. There are no real rules set in stone that say you should post at these times only each day. You've always got to be testing to find what works, and remember, what works now might not work six months from now. For now at least, being on social media at the same time every day is not equivalent to blogging on the same day every week, but because social media is rented land, it's up to you to be on top of how any changes could affect your business.

Although there's really no right or wrong time to post on social media, there are right and wrong things to post at certain times. Here is a perfect example—in March 2017, a prewritten email was scheduled to be sent to help promote our Youpreneur Summit conference, which was taking place in November 2017.

However, on the morning that email was supposed to go out, I turned on the TV and saw on the news that a terrorist act had taken place in London. Somebody had driven a car into a crowd in Westminster. That would have been a bad time to send that email out to my list—not only because some of my audience might have been affected by that tragedy, but also because, from a business perspective, it would have been less likely for someone to click the *buy now* button to purchase tickets to an event being held in a major city where a terrorist attack had just taken place.

I hit the pause button and waited to send that email out until the dust had settled, around two weeks later.

Be mindful of current events, holidays, or happenings beyond your control that can interfere with your audience's ability to engage fully with what you are posting.

The beautiful thing about doing business online is that you're always open for business. We live in a global economy.

It's an exciting time for any entrepreneur anywhere on the planet.

The front door to your business is never closed. It's open 24/7, 365.

A Quick Word on Social Media Etiquette

I will say right now, there is absolutely never any reason to swear in any way whatsoever in anything you do to market your business. Period. You should refrain from using any kind of curse words or any kind of language that might upset even one individual. There's no real need for it.

With that said, and before you start in with the whole, "But so and so does this and they are really successful" bit, I know there are a lot of influencers out there who swear in their marketing all the time. It's part of their brand, and I don't cast

The front door to your business is never closed. It's open **24/7, 365**.

There's a time and place to discuss personal, religious, or political beliefs—and there's a time and place **to just stick to business!**

judgment. Many of them are friends of mine! I just personally believe that you should avoid this as much as possible. I follow this rule myself, and I teach my students inside the Youpreneur Community to do the exact same thing. You'd be amazed how quickly that stuff can spread if it upsets the wrong person, and not in a good way.

You should also avoid saying anything related to religion, unless you are creating a business based around your religious beliefs and your audience is comprised of people who have the same beliefs as you. Religious differences can be polarizing, and when you agitate an audience in that way, you strike nerves that run deep.

Likewise, avoid anything to do with politics. We live in one of the most politically divided times in history. People are more vocal today about how they lean politically than ever before. I believe it's because through social media we all have a platform to voice our opinions. The problem with this is that, especially during an election period, things can get a little heated, and if you're not careful, social communication can get out of hand. We saw this with the 2016 US presidential election.

Holy moly, was social media on fire. I saw a lot of people I respect as business owners and as leaders in their field getting quite abrupt and very vocal about their political beliefs. Even people I never thought would get involved started jumping into the fray. Relationships and partnerships were stressed, and their audiences suffered because of it. It's not that I don't understand—remember, "Brexit" occurred in my home country just months before that election. It's more that I know how deeply and personally we all hold our political beliefs, and I believe two things very strongly: first, that arguing over social media isn't going to change anyone's mind; and second, that arguments are more likely to hurt your business than help it.

You've got to be very careful in regards to what you say on social media.

Make sure conversations you have in any public forum are managed in such a way that your audience as a whole is included in a positive manner.

There's a time and place to discuss personal, religious, or political beliefs—and there's a time and place to just stick to business!

Social media is a huge, ever-evolving group of platforms, and it's definitely proven that it's not going anywhere anytime soon. You certainly should embrace it in your business. Just make sure that you're doing it the right way. Stay relevant in your audience's mind and really focus on no more than three platform profiles that will be the best fit for communicating what you are all about.

What we're doing here, on this part of our journey, is making sure that the foundations are in place. All of this process is at the very core of the Youpreneur ecosystem, which we'll delve into further in future chapters.

CASE STUDY

NAME: Carrie Wilkerson
BUSINESS NAME: The Barefoot Executive
WEBSITE: CarrieWilkerson.com

Background

Carrie Wilkerson began to work at home after the adoption of her two eldest. After doing so successfully, others wanted her to teach them about navigating parenting, being your own boss, productivity, and profitability without going insane.

Establishing Authority

Carrie contributes her success in establishing her authority to showing up consistently, credibly, and helpfully in social media with a professional look and cohesive feel in messaging, colors, and graphics. She has always felt that consistency is the key to establishing any brand.

Other factors for Carrie have been sharing her content through guest blogging, interviews, media, and her book—which she says came as a result of her social media visibility.

Three Things to Grow Business Effectively

1. Sharing content: Carrie creates videos, shows up on interviews, writes blog posts, answers questions in social media, and does her best to stay visible to the public. Carrie knows it's important to show up a little bit everywhere whenever possible.

2. Public speaking has been super helpful for every single business Carrie has owned and grown. She sometimes speaks for leads, sometimes for sales, and now she speaks for a stand-alone fee as an income stream.

3. Targeted advertising: Carrie takes advantage of advertising in the form of either social media ads or content targeted to specific audiences that she wants to reach via a guest blog or guest interview spot.

Most Profitable Monetization

Carrie says that Infoproducts are most likely the most profitable aspect of her business. Infoproducts have not only made her money on their own but have also lead to coaching opportunities and speaking engagements.

Here's what Carrie had to say about what excites her the most about being a personal brand business owner:

I'm responsible for ME—my reputation, my credibility, my energy, and my focus. My brand evolves and changes as I do. Sure, it's not sellable... but that's not really my end game with this business. As my biggest asset, I can always recreate and shift as the market does, making sure I'm on trend, on point, and in demand.

PART 2
MARKETING

5

SPREADING YOUR MESSAGE

I N previous chapters, we've discussed what a Youpreneur needs to know about building a business. We've covered defining who you are and what you want to be known for, as well as what your perfect customer looks like. We've also talked about how important it is to build your online home, start blogging, and set up and utilize your social media platforms the right way.

The question now is—how do you start to spread your message to a wider audience?

This is where it gets fun. In this next stage you get to really focus in and start to market your message. You get to talk about what you want to do and the people you want to serve, and ultimately get those people ready to be brought on board as customers. Today, there are online-savvy consumers ready and waiting to discover you and fall in love with what you're all about. You reach that audience and establish that relationship by experimenting with and utilizing different types of what I refer to as *rich online media*.

We've already touched on blogging, online video, pod-casting, and regular social media interaction as part of getting started with your online home. However, now it's time to spread your message as far and as wide as you can. For that to happen, we've got to take it up a notch.

I want to kick this section off by confirming that getting everything done that we've outlined in the first part of this process—focusing on the first building of your business—is genuinely just the foundation. Getting your website up and running and creating that initial batch of content is only the beginning. To really catapult your brand's message and your overall reach as an influencer, you'll want to build a rich online media experience.

It's this experience that'll truly play one of the biggest roles in helping you to become the go-to source in your industry.

Building a Media Company Mindset

One of the most important things you can do as a wannabe Youpreneur is establish your authority in your niche. The first step to doing that is offering really solid information. I find blog posts, checklists, case studies, and such are, without a doubt, the richest type of media you can share.

At the very center of what you do when it comes to estab-lishing your authority is showing people, time and time again, that you can solve their problems. That is why I continually talk about how-to blog posts and podcast episodes. Your audience has to know that you are the person who can ease the pain points. Your job is to make the process of convincing them that you're the answer to their problems an easy one.

Remember what I talked about earlier on in regards to know, love, and trust? Here's where we really ramp that up. If you want to become a true authority in your niche, you have to get people to fall in love with you as deeply and as quickly as possible.

In reality, you are becoming somebody's favorite, and that's why building a rich media experience is such an important part of the Youpreneur ecosystem.

When creating content, you are the boss. You control the kind of ideas you want to share and how those ideas are conveyed. Think of it as becoming your very own media company. You get the opportunity to become the *go-to* source in your industry through your blogging, your podcasting, and your online videos. You're going to be "top of mind" when people want news, an update, or help with a topic in your niche.

That media company mindset is something I embraced a long, long time ago as I focused on building my own brand and business around my personality and experience. I asked the questions, *What is an authority? Why is becoming an authority important? Who is the actual authority?* Think about how you traditionally receive information. In the television world, the networks control the content. In the book world, it's the publisher who is in charge. In newspaper, magazine, and print media, the editor holds the reins.

By turning yourself into a media company, you instantly assume control over your content and understand what an authority actually is.

An authority is somebody whose opinion about a certain topic is respected and valued, not only within their industry, but also by the people who want to be part of that industry. That's exactly what an authority is.

By turning yourself into a media company, you instantly **assume control** over your content and understand what an **authority** actually is.

The Importance of Originality

At the very core of every successful personal brand business is the all-important decision, made very early on, to be as original as possible. There is a lot of talk today about authenticity, and you certainly want to be as authentic as possible. But I feel that originality is just as important.

Authenticity is being true to yourself, but originality is making that true version of you different from anything else that exists in your niche. You want to be unique. There's the old adage an original is always worth more than a copy, and I agree with that.

In today's easy-to-use Internet universe, people are getting sloppy. They're copying other people's material left and right—podcast formats and blog designs. And sometimes they're not just copying; they're flat out ripping off people's content entirely, word for word, and placing it on their own website or in their e-books or anywhere else they see fit.

Being a Youpreneur means being original in everything you do. You and your experience are one of a kind, and you want to be known for that in your business.

We live in a very smart, tech-savvy, social environment, and people's BS indicators are extremely sensitive. If you blatantly copy someone, people will see it from a mile away and be more than happy to call you out on it, very publicly.

It's Time to Get Personal

Despite all the time and money that goes into branding, people don't choose to do business with a company because of a logo design or a corporate mission statement. They choose to do business with a particular brand because of their own experience with the products or services—and more importantly, because of the people who represent those products and services.

P2P (People to People)

One of the easiest ways I have found to be original is sticking to my relationship-building philosophy of P2P or *people to people.*

I'm an old-school guy who comes from a corporate background. Every job I've ever worked, no matter what position I held, was focused on a B2B (business to business) or B2C (business to consumer) mindset. But I prefer to concentrate on people.

Focus on a P2P relationship philosophy! Why? Because, as you learned earlier, people want to do business with other people!

Your customers want to be your friends. They want to get to know the authority figure behind the business that's taking their money. Most importantly, they want to be treated like real human beings instead of faceless names on invoices. If a customer tweets a company with a question, they want to get a reply in real time, from a real person. The fact that such an interaction is possible is the beauty of today's online content platforms.

Good and Bad P2P

There are two kinds of P2P. There's good P2P, and then there's bad P2P.

Good P2P is getting to know your customers and community members properly by conversing with them via blog comments, answering their questions on Twitter, or hanging out with people who you know follow you at live events. Don't get egocentric and say, "Well, I'm above these people. They read my blog." No. The opposite is true.

Focus on a **P2P** relationship philosophy! Why? Because, as you learned earlier, **people want to do business with other people!**

Spending time **getting to know your customers** better will help them to **fall in love with you** and your message even more easily.

Spending time getting to know your customers better will help them to fall in love with you and your message even more easily.

A great example of good P2P is my favorite fictitious friend, Bob the Baker. When you walk into Bob's bakery, he's already wrapping up your favorite loaf of bread because he knows you— he knows your name, he knows what you like, he knows what you order on a regular basis. You're more likely to walk an extra two to three blocks to get to Bob's bakery, and you even spend a little bit more money on your fresh bread with Bob than you would at a big supermarket chain. Why? Because you've got a relationship with Bob, and it's an original relationship. It's you and Bob. That can't be beaten. That's good P2P.

Bad P2P is dragging a passenger off an airplane when you know every single person on that flight has a smartphone on them. It's the 21st century—are you crazy? That's about as bad P2P as you get. I know people who have been very loyal to United Airlines who are now never going to fly with them again.

Another example of bad P2P is Amy's Baking Company. This company was on Gordon Ramsay's *Kitchen Nightmares* a few years ago. It was the first and only time Gordon Ramsay has ever walked off of a TV program because he just couldn't deal with the people. Amy and her husband were keeping tips from their servers, serving food that wasn't good anymore, and cooking in a kitchen that was a mess. It was a complete nightmare.

When the show aired, what did everybody do in today's very social environment? They went to social media and started hitting them hard. What did Amy and her husband do? They attacked. They didn't say, "You're right, we're wrong. You found us out. We're terrible. We're going to change things." No, they went on the attack and seriously hammered their now former customers. That's bad P2P.

The Power of Showing "Behind the Scenes (BTS)"

Sometimes inspiration can come to you in the most ordinary or mundane moments. Times when you're simply going about your life, not really paying much attention to what's happening around you. This very thing happened to me a few years ago, and I learned an extremely valuable lesson in the process.

What I Learned about BTS from Krispy Kreme

A few years ago my then three-year-old son, Charles, and I walked into a new Krispy Kreme donut shop where I lived in the Philippines. The young lady behind the counter walked over to our table after my son had devoured his donut and asked, "Would your son like to see how we make the donuts?" Charles said, "Yes, I'd love to see that." She took him back to the kitchen with her, put a little hat on him, and showed him how the donuts came out of the machine, went through the hot oil, and got coated with all that sugary goodness. Charles loved it—thought it was great. His tour guide gave him a little green Krispy Kreme balloon and a couple of free donuts to take home.

He slept with the balloon that night.

I videoed bits of that visit on my phone. When Charles fell asleep, I edited the clips, put them together, stuck the video up on my YouTube channel, and wrote a blog post about the experience. You can go to ChrisDucker.com and simply search for "Krispy Kreme," and it'll pop up.

People are more likely to talk about negative experiences than they are positive ones. How messed up is that? That's how we handle customer service. We usually talk when we're upset but not when we're happy. In this case, I talked about having a great customer service experience.

I tweeted it out. I went to bed. I woke up the next morning, and I had a reply back from Krispy Kreme in the United States saying, "Thanks so much for this great video. We're glad you had such a fun time at one of our locations overseas." I was blown away, but I was even more blown away when I found out that Krispy Kreme includes the video from that blog post as part of their franchise training in the country and—get this— the young lady who was our Krispy Kreme guide is now the manager of the location that we visited.

It's no coincidence she's managing that store now. She was promoted because she cared. Caring is at the very center of what customer service is all about and what you need to do above and beyond everything else.

You've got to care about people. It's that simple.

Remember how I said a big part of the rich media you create could be behind the scenes stuff? You may think I have drifted off point, but that whole Krispy Kreme story started when the girl behind the counter asked to show us the *behind the scenes* of the donut-making operation.

The whole concept of behind the scenes is to show somebody how something is done. That's it. But if you care about your customers, it shows that too.

You've got to **care** about people. **It's that simple.**

What I Learned about BTS from Star Wars

One of the reasons I continue to buy Blu-ray DVDs even though I can download the same movies digitally via Amazon, Netflix, or iTunes is that the film companies put "extras" on the DVDs. They know people will buy them because they want to see behind the scenes.

I purchased *The Force Awakens*, the Star Wars movie, on Blu-ray. Honestly, the only real reason I picked up the disc instead of just downloading it was that I wanted to see the behind the scenes stuff. It was well worth it because one of the extras was video of a read-through with all the actors sitting around a table going through the script together. I'm a big Star Wars geek and ate that content up.

Fans want to see what you're doing now to get to where you are going.

It's getting to know you, on steroids.

Take another extra from that DVD—shooting a special Star Wars moment. Harrison Ford walks into the *Millennium Falcon* for the first time in God knows how many years and says to his walking carpet of a faithful sidekick, "Chewie, we're home." If that doesn't give you goose bumps as a Star Wars fan, I don't know what will. But even more importantly, in the extra, we get to see how excited the crew was to have that one line shot for the new film.

This is why behind the scenes is so important. It's showing people how something gets done. And just like the Krispy Kreme BTS, these glimpses can reveal how much the people involved love producing the product, service, whatever for you.

Everyone Loves a Good Car Chase

If you remember, many moons ago, O.J. Simpson got into a white Bronco and took the police on a little bit of a car chase. It was all over TV. It even interrupted prime-time sports, which included the NBA playoffs. Everyone loves a good car chase, but this was the all-time ultimate in behind the scenes. Somebody super famous who is being accused of a horrific crime gets into a car and is driven slowly down the highway with a ton of police cars following. Why do we want to watch it? Because we want to know how it's going to end.

People want to watch as stories unfold. You just have to invite them to follow your story, the story of your brand and your business. Say something like, "I'm going to be holding a great event in November this year. I would love for you not only to be there, but also to follow the journey as my team and I get ready to put on the best live event in our industry."

What are you going to show your BTS followers? You're going to show them round-table meetings. You're going to show them the swag designs you get. You're going to introduce them to your speakers. You're going to show them what the stage looks like before you've got all your branding attached to it and the lights are on it.

People love a good car chase. That's why everybody followed that live news footage of O.J. in the Bronco. It's because we wanted to see how it ended. When you do behind the scenes right, it's some of the most powerful, rich marketing you can possibly get involved with.

How Live Video Changes Everything

Of all the types of content you can create in today's world, video is king. Don't get me wrong; other types of content are necessary too. I love the idea of keeping people up-to-date with my social media and blog posts. But, when we talk about behind the scenes, video really does change everything.

We've talked about evergreen and social video in the first part of the book, but there's another video format that is changing the game entirely. And that's live video.

Now, some might disagree with me on this point. They might say that all social media–based video is "live." But it's not.

The Difference Between Social Video and Live Video

Social video formats like Snapchat or Instagram Stories don't stay around forever. They actually come and go quite quickly. People who are interested in following you behind the scenes and seeing what you're working on have to tune in during a specific time frame. When I put something up on Instagram Stories, for example, I get hundreds and hundreds of people watching what I'm doing just seconds, minutes, or (at the very most) a few hours after it happens.

The difference between social video and live video is the time frame. With live video, you're actually getting people to watch live as you create the video, not seconds, minutes, or a few hours later.

Facebook Live, Twitter's Periscope, and Instagram's live video component all offer the ability to go live and interact with people. The cool thing about doing a live video is that people can show you love while you're creating it. They can tap their screens and give you hearts or a thumbs-up emoji. They're actually engaging with you live on the spot.

This is gold for Youpreneurs. And it's gold for P2P, because you're building those relationships in a very intimate manner, in real time.

And another beautiful thing about live video is when you're done, the video doesn't go anywhere. It stays on your profile, so people who missed it the first time will be able to watch it later, much later even. You can run retargeting adverts to that live video, which enables you to be able to then grow the viewership of that video, and anything that you've discussed in it.

SOCIAL VIDEO	LIVE VIDEO
TWITTER	FACEBOOK
SNAPCHAT	PERISCOPE
INSTAGRAM STORIES	INSTAGRAM LIVE
PERFECT FOR	**PERFECT FOR**
Behind the Scenes	Office Hours Q&A
Short-Form P2P	Slide Deck Training
Reaction Content	Long-Form Presentations
Private Communication	Interview Content

Why You Must Repurpose Your Content

Deciding on which modalities to use to deliver your content is just as crucial as determining how much content to produce and how often. Most business owners assume they know what people want and how they want to receive it. This is called guessing. You may or may not be correct, and unless you have an audience to ask, you won't know either way.

When just starting out, you have to go with what you are most comfortable with. Some people are not comfortable being in front of a camera, so video may not work for them, and that's fine. Maybe they have a really good voice. They could have a great tone and a soothing way of talking people through whatever it is that they want to talk about. If that's the case, then podcasting could be a great modality.

But here's what you have to remember: just like you may be more comfortable delivering content through specific vehicles, your audience also has preferences for how to receive that content. You will find there are subsections of your community that will choose to consume content presented in a particular format over others.

For example, I know there is a portion of my audience that will listen to my podcast but would never read a blog post from me and vice versa. There's also a good chunk of my audience that loves watching my YouTube videos and will consume and share my infographic posts on my website but wouldn't necessarily listen to my podcast. You want to create different types of content as time goes by to really see what hits home better or more effectively for your customers.

You're probably screaming out at me right now saying, *Wait a second there, Chris! You're telling me I have to create all this content in all these formats? How in the world will I be able to do that?* Take a deep breath and relax. This is where repurposing comes in to save the day.

The trick is to create one piece of content and repurpose it into different formats to satisfy the needs of different people.

You're going to create one piece of content that you can use over and over and over again. The best way to do this is to start with video. Once you've got a video of yourself, you can:

- Separate the audio and turn that into a podcast episode.
- Take that audio and extract the five main points and turn it into an infographic.
- Have that video transcribed and turned into a blog post.

The trick is to **create one piece** of content and **repurpose** it into different formats to **satisfy the needs** of different people.

- Cut down that 15-minute video and turn it into lots of one-minute clips to be able to promote the podcast or the blog post on social media.

A perfect example of someone who knows how to do this is my good friend Lewis Howes, who is the main man behind the incredibly popular podcast *The School of Greatness*. He has a book of the same title and is growing an incredible business based around him—his experience, his personality, and the way that he wants to serve other people. Lewis is a Youpreneur on steroids. He's not a writer. He's not a blogger. He creates all his content for his podcast in video first. You may be asking why on earth would he create content for his *audio podcast* in video format. Let me explain.

What's happening is he's creating video content and audio content at the same time. He knows his audience likes to either listen to him or watch him. They simply prefer not to read content, so he has worked out how to satisfy both preferences simultaneously.

This opens a great opportunity to cross-promote both platforms. On the podcast, he'll say, "Hey, go check out this video on my YouTube channel if you like to view content rather than listen to it." On YouTube, he might say, "Hey, if you're on the move and you want to listen to this interview instead of watching it, check out my podcast on iTunes."

What Lewis also does brilliantly is take sections of that video content and break it down into little one-minute clips and then use those on social media—Instagram, Twitter, Facebook—to actually promote the individual podcast episodes.

Lewis is creating his content in a manner that he's really good at, but he also understands the power of different modalities to be able to attract his audience. He's always leading them back to actually consuming his content on one of his two main mediums.

I have used this same strategy for several pieces of content at ChrisDucker.com and Youpreneur.com. I might have a blog post that does really, really well, so I'll turn it into a podcast episode because I know there are podcast listeners who don't read my blog (and vice versa). It's the old adage of hitting a couple of birds with one stone.

This *one-to-many* approach (where you are the one, and your audience is the many) has been one of the key ways that I've been able to grow my authority in my industry and spread my message far and wide, and you can do likewise.

- My Blog: ChrisDucker.com
- My Podcast: *Youpreneur FM*
- My Mastermind Community: Youpreneur.com
- My YouTube channel: YouTube.com/ChrisDucker

All of the online properties listed above serve me well in spreading my message and gaining new followers, subscribers, and customers. To help you develop a solid content marketing strategy so you can do likewise, turn the page for another roadmap you can follow.

Why You Need to Be Remembered

Why are you creating content? It's to be remembered. It's to be seen as the go-to source in your industry—someone who is trustworthy and knowledgeable. You want to be seen as the one person fans, followers, and customers turn to when they need answers, support, motivation, or to simply be entertained.

There's no better way to be remembered than as yourself— and if you follow my P2P philosophy, your personality will clearly shine through in your content. In many ways, the P2P philosophy is the true reason that you're creating content in the

HOW TO DEVELOP AN EVERGREEN CONTENT MARKETING STRATEGY

DEFINING WHO YOU ARE

THE VISION
Lay out a clear idea of your business, your mission, and your voice to give you a clearer sense of how you can serve others.

THE EDGE
Write down what sets your business apart from your competitors and the unique value you provide.

THE OBJECTIVE
Plan out the goals for your content marketing and set benchmarks for you to track your progress against.

TOP TIP: List three brand competitors in your niche and see what they are doing and what they do not offer that you can offer.

DEFINING YOUR TARGET AUDIENCE

SURVEY YOUR AUDIENCE
Narrow down who your customer avatar is for a clearer picture of who you want to be serving and marketing to.

PAIN POINTS
Understand what your audience's problems are and what you can provide them. Those solutions will help set you apart from your competitors.

REACHING YOUR AUDIENCE
Find out where your audience likes to hang out, what kind of content they enjoy, and the best way you can reach them.

PICKING YOUR CONTENT

WRITTEN CONTENT
- Blog posts
- E-books
- Infographics
- SlideShare presentations

AUDIO/VIDEO CONTENT
- Podcasts
- Webinars
- YouTube videos
- Live-streaming videos

PLANNING YOUR CONTENT SCHEDULE

FREQUENCY
Establish how often in a week or month you would like to publish content.

PROCESS
Put a process in place, assigning which member of your team does which task and the lead time it takes to create the content.

PLATFORMS
Map out where you plan on taking your content, whether it's social media, blogs, landing pages, your email list, etc.

IMPORTANT

There are TWO important parts to the success of your content marketing strategy:

1. Listen to your audience. They will tell you what they need help with, where their struggles are, and how you can serve them.

2. Be consistent. The biggest "killer" in content marketing is not consistently publishing high-value content on a regular basis. We want 'em waiting for more from us . . . but not waiting for too long!

If you'd like a really useful Process Blueprint on How to Breathe New Life into Your Content Archive, simply visit the following URL and it's yours, for free: **Youpreneur.com/ ReadersOnly**

first place and working to make it as enduring and evergreen as possible.

Of course, the content required to do this MUST include you—your personality, your stories, and your expertise. People will find you with this content, and you will make an impression upon them. Ultimately, this impression will cause a reaction—or, as it's known in the world of business, a transaction!

CASE STUDY

NAME: Jay Baer
BUSINESS NAME: Convince & Convert
WEBSITE: ConvinceAndConvert.com

Background

Jay Baer started in digital marketing in 1994. He built a digital marketing consultancy that became the largest online agency in Arizona. Jay sold that firm in 2005 and started Convince & Convert in 2008. Since 1994, Jay has advised 35 of the FORTUNE 500 brands, and the Convince & Convert Media division runs a large online magazine, a network of podcasts, courses, and many other resources for mid- and large-company marketers.

Establishing Authority

The Convince & Convert blog (which was formerly written only by Jay) was the first personal brand springboard he used. That was followed by Jay's first book, *The Now Revolution*, written with Amber Naslund, and he also began speaking consistently. The combination of these efforts is what has established Jay as an authority.

Three Things to Grow Business Effectively

1. Jay's blog continues to create significant awareness for him and his firm. However, the content on that blog is by no means solely created by Jay at this point. Jay's team publishes five to 10 posts per week, with one to two of them written by Jay himself. Google organic search accounts for 70 percent of the site's traffic.

2. Jay speaks at 60 events per year and does 25 webinars, creating significant awareness and lead generation.

3. Jay's podcast, *Social Pros*, is approaching 300 episodes. Each show interviews a big-brand social media marketer, and in that way Jay interviews people who would be ideal customers for his consulting business.

Most Profitable Monetization

The content Jay creates for awareness is directly monetized through sponsorships and brand partners. His podcasts, email, blog, webinars, etc., are all sponsored, and mostly by SAAS companies. Sponsorships went from a $0 revenue stream to a seven-figure revenue stream in four years.

Here's what Jay had to say about what excites him the most about being a personal brand business owner:

Customers in every industry trust people far more than they trust companies. Personal brand owners have the ability to create trusted bonds with customers and prospects, and use that "halo effect" to pass that trust along to the rest of their company.

6

POSITIONING YOURSELF AS AN EXPERT

THERE is a lot of talk about building authority and becoming an expert, or guru, in today's information marketing world. It seems that everyone out there has the newest, latest, and greatest way for you to solidify your role as that *go-to* person in your niche. In addition to everything that we've already discussed, I believe there are four main areas that every Youpreneur should zoom in on when it comes to positioning yourself as an expert:

1. Speaking
2. Coaching
3. Being Featured in Traditional Press Outlets
4. Being a Guest on Podcasts

To become an authority or thought leader, you can run a great blog, update social media on a regular basis, do *Ask Me Anything* live videos. You can put together a potential viral infographic or host an event. All of these are great for building authority, but actually being *seen* as an expert is slightly different, and that's what we are going to talk about here.

All the World's a Stage

One of the best ways to build recognition as a Youpreneur is to get involved with public speaking. It allows you to build a profile on "the circuit" in your industry, as well as create opportunities for other business-related activities.

Now, I understand that some of you reading this book have absolutely no desire to ever get up on stage and speak in public. Almost everyone I've come into contact with who feels this strongly about speaking will not be swayed—so, if that's you, feel free to skip the next 1,000 words or so!

However, if you do want to be taken seriously as a potential speaker, and to be booked by both small and large events, you must get your speaker page set up on your website.

Event organizers love to see what you've got to offer to their audience. Show them!

Anyone contemplating booking an expert to come and grace the stage at their event will visit a potential speaker's website to preview how they speak. Event organizers are looking to see if you are the right fit for their audience. You being on their stage, in front of their people, puts them at risk. If you perform well and the crowd loves you, the organizer looks like a hero, but if you tank on stage, it's the organizer who gets the blame.

Ideally, anyone checking out your speaker page will find high-quality photos of you from various speaking gigs, some showing the size of the crowd you're speaking in front of. (Those are always impressive.) But, even if you haven't actually started your speaking career yet, you still need to have a speaking page on your website.

I have seen experts who truly wanted to make speaking part of their overall brand and their business ecosystem hire a photographer to shoot photos of them in various positions as if they were talking to an audience. They are either holding a microphone or they've been mic'd up in some way to make it look like they're speaking. It's not being sneaky or anything, it's just showing people that you are in a position to provide expert advice, and you want to do it from their stage.

Event organizers **love to see** what you've got to **offer to their audience**. Show them!

Event Organizers Love Popcorn (The Showreel)

If you have been speaking for a while and you've got some good, high-quality video of yourself, put together a showreel and have that available on your website. Event organizers love to be able to sit and watch a couple of minutes of you in action—actually onstage in front of a live audience.

If your video clips show you speaking on different topics, that's a plus.

If you don't have a lot of video from stage available, record a short video of yourself talking directly to a camera. Look those event organizers in the eye and tell them exactly what they can expect from you as a speaker. They're your audience, so take care that they fall in love with you!

As you do speaking events, never stop collecting testimonials from event promoters and organizers to highlight on your speaking page.

You can visit my showreel at ChrisDucker.com/Speaking as an example to follow.

To Keynote or Not to Keynote?

Generally, there are two types of speakers, so when you're thinking about building your speaking page, you should figure out whether you want to be known as a keynote speaker or a workshop-style speaker. There is a difference. Keynote speakers tend to be more inspirational, more motivational, and they tell more stories. Workshop-style speakers are more focused on the "how to" element. Chances are you'll probably begin speaking as a workshop speaker. I did. You can always morph into a keynote speaker as time goes by, just as I have myself.

When it comes to building out your speaking page, start with a really nice attention-grabbing headline, and make sure

You're **pitching the people** who could ultimately **introduce you to a new audience.**

you identify for the event organizer the key benefits of having you as a speaker at their event. Remember, you're not pitching to your audience here—they already know, love, and trust you. Your speaking page is written specifically to event organizers and decision makers. And what's more? You're pitching the people who could ultimately introduce you to a new audience.

The crucial thing to remember when building your speaker page is that an event organizer doesn't want to have to figure out how to "fit you in." It's all very well for you to have a great page with an awesome showreel and testimonials, but event organizers are very busy people. They're going to want to know what you can do for them and how you're going to do it.

Come up with two or three keynote session titles that you can speak on. Those titles, with some quick descriptions as to what those sessions actually include, are a necessity for your expert speaking page.

As you start getting booked, it is also good to show a list of your upcoming speaking engagements because this will offer social proof that you are in demand. Please don't forget to include a way for prospective clients to contact you directly on this page. Don't assume they will look for your *contact us* on another page on your site. Make it easy for them to find out how to get in touch with you.

If you don't have some of the materials I have talked about, don't fret. Collect them as you go, and continue adding them to your speaking page. While we're on the subject of speaking, allow me to share a few quick tips that I've picked up through the years that I hope you'll find useful.

Quick Speaking Tips Learned in the Trenches

First up, the air inside most venues is dry, and if you haven't done a lot of speaking before, you may not be used to how the air can affect your voice over a long presentation. Bring something right up on stage with you to eliminate any embarrassing coughing fits—a bottle of room-temperature water is my jam on this one! Cough drops work well too.

Next, let's talk about the audience. Being on stage can be intoxicating. You may want to make incredible statements that apply to everyone in the room; however, your talk will have a lot more impact if you make repeated eye contact with just a few people and speak directly to them. This will not only make the experience feel more like a conversation than an official presentation, but it'll have the added bonus of making your audience nod along in agreement as you go. Try it... it REALLY works.

And lastly, don't forget to keep the conversation going after your talk.

Your audience is there to hear you speak and learn more about you, so do them the favor of making it easy to find you after the presentation is over. At the very least, add a finishing slide to your presentation with your social handles and website. If you want to take it up a notch, add a special bonus offer for anyone who was there to see you live. This focuses on creating even MORE value and converting them to your email list at the same time! And to deliver the ultimate value bomb, stick around after your presentation to have conversations with the audience. This is the P2P magic that can't be replicated, so build it into your speaking schedule if at ALL possible!

For more information on how to actually prepare for a speaking gig, visit ChrisDucker.com/Speaking-Gig for a short video jammed with tips!

Aligning Yourself with the "Traditional" Press

This is a bit of a weird one because all press, I believe, is new media press nowadays. Most longstanding newspapers and magazines have an online presence. Even the *New York Times* charges for an online subscription. Whatever form they may be publishing in, traditional press outlets, meaning respected outlets, can boost your expert status if they happen to feature you or your business.

The easiest way to catch the attention of the traditional press is to just tell your story. Remember what we talked about a little earlier on?

You are 100 percent original. There is only one you. That's why you're building The Business of You. You're building the business around you, and your brand, and the people who you want to serve.

You've got an interesting story behind you! You've got to figure out the best way to tell it.

Sharing Social Proof

The goal here is to be able to say on your website *as seen in*, or *as seen on*, or *featured in* and then display the logo or icon of *Entrepreneur* magazine, or *Inc.* magazine, or *Forbes*, or *Huffington Post*, or whatever the publication is. That's being *seen* as an expert. The easiest way to get the ball rolling is to contact the journalists and contributors of those outlets and say something like this to them: *Hey, I've got a great story on how I beat burnout and tripled my business's income the following year. Who doesn't want to hear that story? I've got a great story on how I went through back surgery because I was sitting at a desk for 15 hours a day, but now I'm only working seven hours a day and I'm fitter and healthier than ever.*

That's a great story—just tell your story.

You've got an **interesting story behind you!** You've got to **figure out the best way to tell it.**

Ninja Tip: On social media, follow the publications you'd like to be featured in and the journalists who write for them. They're *always* looking for great stories, and they are often posting in search of angles, hooks, stories, and interview sources. Soon enough, you'll learn who writes about the kinds of things you excel in and which outlets publish the stories you have to tell. Build relationships with them over time, and be first to respond when they put out a call for stories in your niche. More about this... right now, below.

Playing the PR Long Game

When it comes to aligning yourself with the press, it's very important to play the PR long game. These guys don't know you from Adam. You might actually have to have several contacts with them before they give you a break and tell your story on their outlet or website. Don't think it's going to be overnight or that one connection will all of a sudden get you on major media networks. It can take some time to build up enough rapport and trust for them to offer to run your story.

One of the easiest ways to get on the good side of a journalist is to simply offer help. Offer them support where you can. *I saw that you wrote an article on A, B, C (subject matter) last week. I also know somebody who could help you with a follow-up article and this is their contact information.* Or, *I saw that you're writing a series on X, Y, Z (subject matter again). I'd like to be able to help you out with some quotes and some resources.*

Journalists are very busy people, and they're almost always on a deadline. Offering help to them on an ongoing basis will work wonders to build a relationship that leads to the kind of exposure you're looking for.

Play the PR long game, and sooner or later, they'll start showing you some love.

Want Massive Reach? Enter the Podcast!

Podcasting is huge. It's the 21st-century Internet radio revolution! There isn't anything more intimate, in my mind, for getting your message across than somebody physically inserting an earbud into each side of their head and listening to you talk. It's about as personal as it can get.

I believe that every Youpreneur has a podcast in them.

However, in the world we do business in today, getting recognized as an expert means being interviewed by *other* influencers on *their* podcasts. These other people have audiences. They've already built communities based on what they do and what they're known for. And the easiest way to get a feel for podcasting is to become a podcast guest yourself.

When seeking to be a guest on a podcast, take careful aim and make sure you are focusing on the right targets. The mistake I see a lot of people make is going at it as if they were on an AK-47 type of mission. They just squeeze the trigger and throw all these bullets around all over the place, hoping to get on as many shows as possible. That's not the right way to do it.

What you want to be is more of a sniper. You want to hone in on the target and strategically aim, making sure you're getting on the right shows for you, because otherwise, you're just wasting your time. Here are a few tips on how to become a great podcast guest, and more importantly, how to pitch yourself as such.

Be a Fan First

You wouldn't believe how many pitches podcast hosts get from people who don't even listen to their podcast. I get them literally every single day. It's painfully obvious when I'm receiving a long-form email or a blanket pitch that has been sent to a dozen other hosts. I promise you those are always the first I delete. I'm just not interested at all.

Don't ever consider pitching a podcast that you haven't heard at least a handful of episodes of yourself!

Good hosts work hard to create valuable content for their specific audience, and you really have no business being on a show if you aren't part of that audience.

Don't ever consider **pitching a podcast** that you haven't heard at least a **handful of episodes** of yourself!

Do Your Research

A lot of podcasts will have sites or at least a page on their website dedicated to their podcast. Even if you already listen to the show regularly, check out that information. See if the host has any requirements for potential guests or guidelines to follow once you have been invited to be on the show. If you don't have a relationship with the host already, this is a way for you to get to know them and educate yourself about their show.

Personalize Your Pitch

Instead of creating a long-form, boring letter pitching how great you are, focus in on making your appearance on their podcast a no-brainer. This means going the extra mile to make your email really intriguing. Personalize your email to show how your message will add value to the host's show and how it will impact their audience.

- You have to be bright.
- You have to be brief.
- You have to show your confidence.
- You have to show your expertise.

Your introduction email should be no longer than 200 words—that's the max. You just need a couple of short paragraphs that include a quick greeting, a little bit of information about your expertise, and some kind of demonstration or proof that you actually listen to the show. You can comment on a joke the host told or mention a story that they talked about on a recent episode. This makes the email more personal and hits that button much quicker than just saying, "Episode 60 was the best one I've ever heard."

You then have to include an invitation for the host to check out a piece of content that you've already created. This is the biggie. You could send them to a blog post, a video, a podcast, or maybe even an infographic. Whatever it is, make it something that could ultimately lend itself to a really interesting discussion for their audience.

Bring Them Back for the After-Party

As the interview wraps up, you will be seen as the expert in your niche. This is a great time to invite everyone listening back to your place of business. At the end of the interview, your host will, nine times out of 10, give you an opportunity to talk about one thing you're working on. Many times they'll even endorse it for you. They'll talk about a book or product that you might be launching.

You've got to use this time very wisely.

State briefly what you'd like the listeners to know about, why it's important for them to know about it, and add in one or two little bonus "value bombs" toward the end. Make it clear what you want them to do. Don't beat around the bush here; you have to convince the listeners that it's both valuable and important that they take action now.

Give one very specific website address for people to go to. Just one!

This should be a site with information on what you're all about and how you can further serve them. I cringe when I hear a guest say something like, "Well, thanks for having me on the show. You can find out more about me on my site, and here's where you can find my book, and if you want to connect on social media, you can find me here."

No. Stop it already! The listener is not going to go to all those places to find you. Simply say, *Thanks for having me on the show; it was a real pleasure, and if anyone wants more information about me and what I'm all about, they can just go to ChrisDucker. com. I've got links there to everything I'm working on.* One website. One call to action.

Give **one very specific** website address for people to go to. **Just one!**

Once the show is over, there will be a great opportunity to practice the P2P philosophy I discussed earlier. You want to build relationships with these other influencers. This is not a *one podcast interview and done* strategy. Follow up with the show host. Immediately write them a thank-you email and say, "That was a lot of fun. I really enjoyed it. I hope it was what you were looking for. Thanks again for having me on." As a closing brownie-point-gaining action, promise to promote the show on your platform when it comes out.

Remember to be the person who enjoys your relationships and growing them—not just "using them" for your own advantage.

Everything I have talked about in this chapter comes down to being yourself. And that's what I've been talking about through the entire book. No smoke and mirrors here. If you want to become an authority, and if you want to be seen as an expert, you tell your story. There's only one you. The original truly *is* worth more than a copy.

CASE STUDY

NAME: Jeff Goins
BUSINESS NAME: Goins Enterprises
WEBSITE: GoinsWriter.com

Background

Jeff Goins has been writing his whole life but always thought about it as a hobby, a creative outlet if you will. Then in 2010, a friend asked what his dream was and Jeff said it was to be a writer. "You don't have to want to be a writer, Jeff," his friend said. "You are a writer. You just need to write." The next day, Jeff started his blog.

Establishing Authority

The first thing Jeff did was write every day without fail for an entire year. Granted, that may not work as a marketing strategy today as well as it did before, but Jeff wasn't doing it for the exposure. Jeff was doing it for the practice. Doing your work in public is the best way for people to see what you can actually do.

Second, Jeff started guest posting, and this was, hands down, the best way to grow his brand. Placing his content strategically in other channels where people could find his work helped him build his audience off of other people's audiences and solidified his reputation as an authority.

Three Things to Grow Business Effectively

1. Jeff writes books. This generates revenue, but it also helps spread his audiences beyond the reach of his own influence. Readers become fans, and fans become customers.

2. Jeff writes articles. As a writer, the best promotion of his work is the work itself, whether that's publishing on his own site or

on someone else's. Jeff writes at least a couple of new pieces every week that get published in a variety of places.

3. Jeff speaks. This works two different ways: Jeff attends a number of events around the world each year that feature him as a keynote speaker, but he also leads webinars almost on a weekly basis. Collectively, these experiences have put him in front of hundreds of thousands of people and sold millions of dollars in products.

Most Profitable Monetization:
Jeff says that building online courses based on his audience's needs and desires has been the most profitable part of his business.

Here's what Jeff had to say about what excites him the most about being a personal brand business owner:

I get to show my kids what a life of freedom, passion, and abundance truly looks like.

7

GROWING YOUR BUSINESS CIRCLE

HERE'S a truth in business that's often overlooked: Your business will only grow to the size of your current circle. You have access to a certain audience, and unless you actively and purposefully grow that audience, you will never get your message in front of new prospects.

You may be thinking, *Chris, are you saying that my business will never grow bigger than it currently is?* Absolutely not, but I am saying you have to be proactive. You have to extend your reach to gain access to more people in order to grow. There are a lot of different ways that you can grow your business circle, but I want to touch on a couple of the more effective ones for Youpreneurs:

- Aligning Yourself with Other Experts
- Attending Live Events
- Investing in Yourself

Aligning Yourself with Other Experts

Growing your circle really begins with the people you choose to surround yourself with. Motivational speaker Jim Rohn said that you are the average of the five people you spend the most time with. Let's just pause there for a second. That's huge. That's really, really important to understand. The five people who you interact with the most have a profound influence on you. If you're surrounding yourself with people who aren't on board with what you're all about, you're swimming upstream against a pretty powerful current straight away.

If you surround yourself with people who understand what you're all about, you will find it much easier to navigate the waters of success!

I would even take it one step further and say you should surround yourself with people who have more experience than you. You never really want to be the smartest person in the room or on the call.

But, you shouldn't build relationships with other influencers just because you want to get access to their email list, or because you want to be on their podcast, or because you want to get invited to the live event that they're holding. This is about building real relationships, ones that will develop over a number of years.

Relationships should be treasured, not used.

One of my biggest pet peeves is when a person I barely know asks me to promote their product. I met them five minutes ago, and they want me to help them sell something because they know that I've got a good-sized email list. That's somebody who is simply out to use relationships. It doesn't go down very well with me at all. I think you'll find that it won't go down with anybody else either. Take the time to really get to know the person you're wanting to align yourself with.

If you **surround yourself with people who understand what you're all about**, you will find it much easier to navigate the waters of success!

Relationships should be **treasured**, not used.

A long-term relationship fosters long-term success, but burnt bridges can never be crossed again.

Align yourself with the type of influencers you want to become known for hanging out with, but do it for the right reasons. One of the best ways to build close relationships with people is to get to know them on a personal level.

Start off by putting together a list of maybe four or five people in your industry who you would like to build a deep, long-lasting relationship with. You may know all or some of the people on this list already and want to take those relationships up a notch. Or maybe you've never met or spoken to these people before, but you want to start building a relationship with them. Whatever the case may be, write their names down.

Once you have the list, start figuring out what those five people are up to and how you can help. How can your expertise directly benefit them? Maybe they've got a problem they're struggling with and you can provide a solution.

The important thing is to make sure you're genuine about wanting to build a real relationship. How do you make that type of personal connection? One way is to understand that pen and paper still work. In fact, I use this strategy quite often. I have plain white postcards printed with my Chris Ducker logo centered at the top. That's it. There's nothing else on either side. No corny photos, or slogans, or anything like that. It's just a simple card with my logo at the top. I use these to handwrite messages to people.

OMG... Chris, please tell me you're not talking about real mail with stamps and everything! That's exactly what I'm talking about. I quite regularly send these postcards to people, and you should too. Sometimes, at conferences, I will have a batch of these cards in my bag, and when I meet someone for the first time, if I've had an enjoyable dinner with them or if I enjoyed that short coffee meeting we had in the corridor, I'll write them a quick message on one of the cards. Then I take it to the concierge's desk at the hotel and say, "I'm not sure what room Mr. Smith is in, but could you please make sure that he gets this from me?" People remember this kind of stuff. Following up doesn't always have to be via a tweet or via an email; as a matter of fact, it sometimes shouldn't be.

That personal touch can mean a lot in developing the relationships that will obviously help grow your circle and your business for years to come.

Attending Live Events

The second way to grow your circle is to attend live events. I love live events.

I want to build relationships with handshakes and hugs.

From time to time, I might even include a bit of kissing on cheeks because I'm English, and we like to do that every now and then! You want to get to the point where you are with the people you want to be close to, and I mean with them *in person.*

We live in a very fragmented world, and particularly when building an online business, it's actually quite lonely sometimes. As an entrepreneur, you are on your own a lot, and it's nice to be able to get to live events to hang out with people. So build relationships with handshakes, hugs, coffee meetings, dinners, even running around in the gym first thing in the morning. Just get out and be social.

Not all live events are created equal, so choose very carefully. They cost money. Whenever you go to an event, it's more than just the ticket to the event that you're buying. You also have travel fare, hotel costs, and food costs.

One strategy I would suggest is staying away from the huge industry events in the beginning. Work on building relationships with people at smaller events instead. The people who you want to bring into and expand your business circle will likely attend the smaller events as well as the big ones, but they'll be easier to find at smaller events.

I want to **build relationships** with **handshakes and hugs**.

Another reason you need to carefully choose which events you attend is time. Time is our most valuable commodity as entrepreneurs. When you commit to attending a conference, you're devoting two or three days to being at the event and a couple traveling to and fro—that's a week of your life. You're giving up a week of working on your business that you'll never get back again. You've got to choose wisely not only because of the money investment, but also because of your time investment.

When you attend a live event, leave the people you meet with a strong positive first impression. That means there are a few things to avoid.

Number one—don't be that person who doesn't buy a ticket to the event but who walks around the corridors, goes to all the networking get-togethers, and hangs around the lobby trying to grab people's attention. That's annoying at best, and you certainly don't want to be known as that person.

Number two—even if you buy a ticket to the event, don't just walk into rooms and start throwing around business cards like ninja stars! Take the time to meet people before you deal out your contact information. I will not likely keep a card from someone that just walks up and hands it to me without any background or knowledge of who that person is.

Number three—avoid alcohol at live events. You don't need it. A glass of wine at dinner might be okay, but you don't want to be the person who gets drunk and makes an idiot of themselves at the network gathering in the bar. That person doesn't build strong, long-lasting relationships with real players; they just get labeled as someone to avoid. That's not who you want to become.

Investing in Yourself

I believe that even leaders need to follow other leaders in order to continue to grow. That could be a tongue twister, but nonetheless I'm a big believer in it.

Personally, I find myself aligning with slightly older, more experienced men. That doesn't mean that women have got nothing to offer me. I have worked very closely with many female entrepreneurs, coaches, and consultants, and I've learned a heck of a lot from them. However, as I've gotten older and advanced in my career, as well as at home as a father and a husband, I tend to find myself being drawn toward being coached and mentored by slightly older men in my industry.

I'm very blessed to be able to call several big influencers in the online business world my mentors. Some of those relationships are more casual, while some are more structured, with regular calls to each other. Some don't even know it's happening, quite frankly. It's just because I'm watching, and I'm learning from them. The point is, find the leaders in your industry and invest in what they have to offer, then leverage that into building a bigger, better relationship with them in the future.

I not only like to align myself with the right influencers and the right authorities in my industry—I also want to get to know them intimately. One of the best ways you can do that is to get involved in masterminds.

A mastermind is a group of usually no more than four to six people who get together on a regular basis. These get-togethers could be either in person or virtual, using some form of video conferencing service.

People come together in a mastermind group to talk about what they're working on, what their struggles are, what their ideas are, what projects they're planning. Often, there's a hot seat involved, where a member presents to the group what they are working on, and the group then gives feedback and input to help them along.

The fact is, masterminds are huge. They are a great way to take relationship building to a whole new level—as well as the perfect way to invest in yourself, as a leader, in an ongoing way. They make the relationships you're building and treasuring now even deeper because once you share your ideas and your strategies with someone else, that establishes a strong and trusting connection. I have formed and grown some of my closest relationships by interacting as part of a mastermind group.

The benefits of being in a mastermind are so huge that I wanted to share them with as many people as possible. It was for this very reason that I founded the Youpreneur Community. And now we have hundreds and hundreds of entrepreneurs all over the world with close relationships as a direct result of meeting inside of the community—that makes me a happy founder!

Five Ways to Develop Successful Relationships

In my 24-plus years in the business world—the last 12 of which have been as an entrepreneur—I've come to the conclusion that one of the key factors separating the struggling from the ultra-successful is the ability to create, cultivate, and develop successful relationships.

As much as we enjoy hearing about the "self-made" man or woman, the reality is actually pretty clear.

Collaboration and connection will always play a role in our success.

Bottom line: without others, dreams remain dreams.

That means whatever you're pursuing, whatever you're wanting, whatever's keeping you awake at night because you just can't stop dreaming about it... you're going to need to enlist the help of others to get it. However, before you begin making a list of everyone you plan on recruiting to help and what you need from them, I suggest you continue reading first.

Collaboration and connection will **always play a role** in our success.

1. Have a Long-Term Mindset

This may sound a bit counterintuitive, especially for new entrepreneurs who feel a strong sense of urgency, but having a long-term perspective on your relationships will set you up for future success.

This means you don't change who you are to please someone. True relationships are built upon honesty and integrity (you know, all that good stuff our mums taught us!). And accept the fact that relationships go through seasons and evolve. This means understanding that sometimes you'll be close with someone, and other times you'll find you're not speaking to each other for weeks, or even months. But the best relationships—the ones that stand the test of time—are those that you are able to pick up right where they left off (which means not getting butt-hurt if someone doesn't get back to you!).

Value your current relationships. It's easy to take our current relationships for granted and always be about cultivating new ones, but you'll find that successful people have deep relationships that have been cultivated over years of mutual investment. Simply put, remind yourself this is life, and the relationships you build will be with you for a long, long time.

2. Put a Premium on Developing Yourself

As you build your network, never forget that you are also a part of other people's networks too. So with that in mind, *What value do you bring to your network? Have you made a choice to continually grow? Are you trying to take more than you give?*

Successful people like to be around successful people. If you plan on finding yourself inside one of these social circles, it's important to have something of value to contribute.

Just look at the Instagram feed of any celebrity or successful entrepreneur, and you'll see the comments are filled with people who are trying to get something from them. Now think about how that same celebrity or entrepreneur goes to work every day and collaborates with other people who have developed their skills and provide something of value. Let's face it, developing skills takes time. It's not easy, but it's a surefire way to finding yourself in the company of success.

3. Seek to Give More Than You Receive

If you've spent any time following entrepreneurs online, then you've probably stumbled across my good friend, the aforementioned Lewis Howes, host of the wildly popular *The School of Greatness* podcast.

As you read in the Foreword, Lewis began his rise to entrepreneurial success by choosing to host an enormous number of networking events. His mindset was that if he could help connect others and shake as many hands as possible, his life would be enriched. He began from a place of giving. Lewis was not concerned about profiting from these events or seeing what others could do for him. He simply wanted to be a connector of people.

Let's not forget, the path of entrepreneurship is built upon the economic concept of providing value to your customers and prospects. Think of it simply as solving a problem. And this approach applies to relationships, too.

4. Develop a P2P Mindset (As you can tell, I really believe in this!)

People are people. They are not followers. They are not stats. They are not open-rates. They are not subscribers. If you approach your relationship building from a more intimate philosophy, or, as you've heard me call it, the People to People (P2P) mindset, you'll find yourself establishing more meaningful and lasting relationships.

Never underestimate the value of a sincere "Thank You" or "I'm Sorry" to your clients, guests, or team members.

Always thank your staff for what they do. The verbal affirmation is just as important as compensation—something I go into great detail about in my book *Virtual Freedom*. Remember the special moments of someone's life with a simple phone call or card. In the business of building relationships, it's truly the little things that make the biggest difference.

5. Be Intentional with Your Actions

Nothing great happens by accident. It's always intentional—always! Despite having a jam-packed schedule, I make it a priority to connect with my network and staff on a personal

Never under-estimate the value of a sincere **"Thank You"** or "I'm Sorry" to your clients, guests, or team members.

level. This can be as simple as an email thanking a member of my team for helping to wrap up a project ahead of deadline or as detailed as having a baby shower gift sent to someone in my network.

Either way, it's intentional—which means planned and executed. Thanks to today's online tools, it's much easier to do this type of thing than you probably think.

People have picked up sloppy habits when it comes to developing the right type of friendships. They take people for granted, and as a result, get confused when those they thought were their "friends" let them down in one way or another. Don't let that happen to you. Be the person who enjoys your relationships and growing them—not just using them for your own advantage.

Building my business circle is something that never ends for me. I do admit, though, it's not as much of a focal point for me as it was five to seven years ago. I mean, how many friends do we REALLY need, right?! However, investing in real relationships is something that has clearly helped me build my brand, my business, and my worth as an expert in my industry.

I'm pretty sure it'll serve you equally as well.

CASE STUDY

NAME: Jeff McMahon
BUSINESS NAME: Total Body Construction
WEBSITE: TBC.fit

Background
Jeff went to school to be a surgeon, but he was colorblind so he was told he wasn't allowed to go to med school. Around that same

time his mom had a stroke and lost the use of the left side of her body. Jeff got into personal training soon after college to help his mother continue her journey of rehab and conditioning. Jeff fell in love with training and found this was his true calling. Jeff has a degree in pre-med/pre-pharm and is dual certified in exercise science and sports medicine. He is also an orthopedic rehab specialist and a lifestyle wellness coach. Jeff has been doing this for over 10 years and has worked with over 800 individuals.

Establishing Authority

Jeff's niche is training successful online entrepreneurs. The first thing that helped him establish authority in his space was leverage. Jeff landed Pat Flynn as a client, and worked with him for free (for a period of time) to prove his worth. After that Pat gave Jeff permission to use his testimonial to attract other successful online entrepreneurs.

The second thing that helped Jeff was learning the importance of social media and how to create content and engaging challenges and contests, and be more active with comments and engagement. Jeff tries to be on as many podcasts as possible to spread his message to other people's audiences.

Three Things to Grow Business Effectively

1. Jeff set up a killer website that is attractive, new, and clean looking. When people go to his site, they're always impressed by what they see. He feels your website is important because it is a reflection of you, especially in the online world.

2. Jeff gets on as many podcast shows as possible to reach out to other people's audiences and provide value to them. This way they can learn more about what he does and how he is

there to answer questions and guide them to a healthy lifestyle. Podcasts are becoming incredibly popular, and with so many shows out there with such unique audiences, you can be precise with who you are speaking in front of. Jeff mostly targets business shows to explain how being active and healthy can lead to more business, more energy, and more enjoyment of the success they are building with their business.

3. Jeff attends conferences that are valuable and related to his market. Jeff works with online entrepreneurs, so he attends a lot of podcasting, business, and social media conferences. He feels when going to conferences, you can't be shy. If you go just for the information, that's fine, but you are missing the most important part. Jeff goes to network. Networking has brought Jeff from five figures a year to well into the six figures and more.

Most Profitable Monetization

Building passive income through courses and collaborations has been the most profitable thing for Jeff than anything else. Jeff is in the service industry so trading time for money is great when getting started, but the real growth comes from expanding out from that. Jeff is building courses, doing workshops, and collaborating with others to split revenue on projects.

Here's what Jeff had to say about being a YOUPRENEUR:

It has helped me through the extremely well-done library of content that I can search for roadmaps on how to do any process for my business. The mastermind calls with Chris are priceless, because it's time with an expert on business that you can't get for that price anywhere else! And the community of knowing each other when we go to events makes things even better.

8

GETTING SERIOUS ABOUT GROWING YOUR EMAIL LIST

A s your business grows, you'll try lots of different strategies for building your email list. However, one thing will remain the same—the importance of focusing on building it.

Growing your email list has got to be a constant and central activity when expanding your online business. If it's not, you're ultimately going to fail. You could still make a little money here and there and maybe even build up some notoriety, but at the end of the day, *the money is in the list*. It has been like that for a long, long time, and it will continue that way.

In fact, even with all the bells and whistles of Facebook ad retargeting and advancements in social media platforms, whenever I speak to anybody who takes their online platform and marketing seriously, they always come back to email. It's the staple not only for getting helpful information to your tribe on an ongoing basis, but also for staying in touch with them about your offerings—offerings they need in order to find the right solutions to their problems.

Earlier on in the book, I touched on creating an opt-in magnet when I talked about building your online home. Now, we're going to dive deeper and look at a few different ways you can put your email list growth in the stratosphere, creating what I refer to as the *Prospect Qualification Roadmap*.

Revisiting the Power of the Quick Win

It all comes back to the power of the quick win. People want results, but they don't want to work to find them. That's the problem.

The "quick win" is all about delivering a solution to help somebody solve a problem fast!

As a business owner, you are a marketer, and you should always be marketing, whether via email, or social media, or your blog. It's your job to figure out what people's biggest problems are and then create solutions to solve those dilemmas. If you do that for the people on your email list, giving them one win after another, they're more likely to fall in love with you, and also to continue opening your emails.

I was talking with a client of mine, William, not so long ago. He's in the financial services industry. William came to me with an opt-in problem. He said, *Chris, I don't know what to do. I need your help. I'm in one particular niche, but I'm serving three quite different clients that will all ultimately become the same client further down the line.*

He's got his perfect customer defined quite clearly. However, when people come to him for personal financial advice, they are at three very different stages in their journey. That's actually a good thing, because he can take them on that journey and hold their hand, from one stop to the next, but it does pose some challenges.

Here's how William's audience breaks down. Some people come to him because they're having problems with debt or saving money. Another group comes to him for help getting started with investing. The third type of prospect wants ongoing financial management and consulting.

The **"quick win"** is all about **delivering a solution** to help somebody **solve a problem fast!**

William wanted to make sure that he was giving his audience real value with his opt-in, but if his potential clients were facing different types of problems, how could he offer an opt-in that would give them all a solution?

It was clear William needed to get a little bit more ninja with the way he was approaching this. My suggestion to him was to create three different quick-win opt-in magnets. William decided on the following:

1. 5 Quick Ways to Get Out of Debt (e-book)
2. The Beginner's Guide to Investing (PDF Checklist)
3. Money Management 101 (e-book)

If you only have one opt-in magnet on offer, you have to manually segment your list at some point to best serve your customers and prospects—because just like William's audience, your prospects are also at different places along the journey when they arrive at your site for the first time.

By offering multiple types of opt-in offers, you allow people to choose whichever is the most relevant to them and their *current* problem, which means more people sign on.

At the exact same time, that choice is also "qualifying" them as to where they are in the journey that they're going on with you, which means you can create more relevant content for them and move them to the next part of the journey much faster... and that part could very well have a product and a price tag on it!

The best part of this strategy for William was that it allowed him to track and test his opt-in magnets to see which was most attractive to his audience. He created three different landing pages and ran traffic from Facebook ads to each of them so he could track which was the most popular out of the lot. He then knew which problem the *majority* of people who came to his site were trying to solve. He could still continue to qualify people by offering them the other two opt-ins as well, but now he was able to focus the bulk of his time catering to his largest niche.

That might sound a little complicated, but it's actually very simple to implement because all you need are three opt-in magnets, three landing pages for them to sit on, and a way to collect email addresses. One of the coolest advantages of this approach is that you don't have to worry about segmenting your email list later as you get further down the line because it'll already be done.

My client loved this solution. He became a fan of Chris Ducker for life because not only did it help him grow his very qualified and dedicated lists, but it also helped him monetize them a lot faster.

That's the power of a quick win!

The Qualification Product

After your audience opts in, you'll want to further qualify them. Getting people to move from opt-in prospect to paying customer is a process, and here's where we'll create a "next step" product. That product, nine times out of 10, will be rich media content in some way, shape, or form. I like to use videos for this part of the roadmap. I find them to be the most effective form of media for my clients at this point in our relationship.

Let's stick with William and his financial services industry as an example. He has people opting in to three different lead magnets. One for saving and debt management, one for investing, and the third one for ongoing money management. People are continually opting in to one of those three lists. Day in, day out.

From here, he would create a video series for each of those groups that takes them to the next level. You go from creating a fan by initially solving a problem and giving them the quick win with your opt-in, to now creating a superfan, and the next step from superfan is customer.

You have to dive deeper and expand on your original quick-win product. The quick win gave the prospect enough information to move forward. This next step is meant to really show them the kind of impact you can have on their life if they go in further with you. You've got to show you can help them in a bigger way with your (in this case) video series.

And here's the really exciting bit about all this—you can even charge for your next-step magnet.

Some people like to call this a "trip wire" product. I don't like to use that term. It's just too sleazy and salesy sounding for me. I prefer to call it the "qualification product."

A qualification product should be offered at a low cost, and it should take whatever solution you're providing up a notch or two. This moves the prospect from the free quick win to a small investment. It also verifies that this person will spend at least *some* money with you, so there's a good chance they will be willing to spend more with you in the future.

You want to get this next-step magnet into the hands of your new subscriber as soon as possible after that first contact. They've opted in, they've gotten your initial opt-in magnet for free, and now, you want to wait a few days before you offer them the qualification product.

Don't overthink the creation process of the qualification product. Just continue to solve the problem!

People often get hung up on what to offer. I keep it simple. I always go for three videos. I think it's nice to be able to have a beginning, a middle, and an end to any type of coaching. These videos don't have to be very long. They can be 15 to 20 minutes each. Make them high impact, high value, and high quality. You should be looking to create about an hour's worth of video content in total.

Don't overthink the creation process of the qualification product. Just **continue to solve the problem!**

For William, his first group of prospects would be most attracted to training that will help them not only get out of debt, but also get on the road to saving money on a daily, weekly, or monthly basis.

For his second level of prospects, he could offer a series of videos that not only gets them started with investing, but also moves them to the point where they're making their first five figures a month with their portfolio.

And for his final group of audience members, he can show off his expertise as a financial services legend by offering them

a series on developing high-level habits to manage their financial growth effectively over a three-year period, for example.

PROSPECT QUALIFICATION ROADMAP

The Community Challenge

Another way I like to take my email lists to the next level is
by offering some kind of a community challenge. This has the
ability to go somewhat viral pretty quickly if you do it right. In
a community challenge, you bring lots of people together in
one particular online location for a specific amount of time and
challenge them all to perform the same activity to achieve the
same result.

A perfect challenge example would be learning how to build an email list. Let's say you have a blog or a podcast you're using to teach people how to build their online platform. One of the things you're going to have to teach them is exactly what I'm discussing right now. They'll have to get serious about growing their email list.

Why not have a 30-day challenge where, throughout the course of the 30 days, you offer regular training sessions, giving the members steps to take and challenging them to take massive action? These trainings can be live or recorded. They could be video, audio, or just written emails that go out at regular intervals throughout the challenge timeline.

It doesn't really matter how you deliver the training; the point is to offer it regularly throughout the course of that 30 days. The benefit of having people participate together—with you and each other—is it builds a community where everyone has the support they need to work toward their common goal and there is a sense of accountability.

The overall result, or the target that you want everybody to achieve, could potentially be getting their first 100 email subscribers. A specific goal is important. What happens then is you are not only helping people get to a finish line as a group, but by getting them there, you're also creating a bit of fandom too.

You'll be seen as the hero for bringing everyone together on their mission!

The timing is key with this particular type of email-list growth tactic. Too long a timeline, and it's hard to keep people engaged; too short, and you may find it hard to solidify the community feel you're wanting to create for everyone. I personally like to try and keep these challenges around 10 days. It's a 10-day challenge to do X, Y, Z.

If you really wanted to put this strategy into overdrive, you could create a private Facebook group where everybody who's opted into the challenge is then invited to engage in instant dialog. This helps to build out the accountability for everyone. Members of the group are not only working through the material you're providing them as part of the challenge, but now they're chatting with each other about their journey as well.

They can discuss their wins, their struggles, and even how they overcame those struggles. They can reach out to the community for help or to discuss where they are at that point in the challenge or share what their numbers are like.

All of that creates additional awareness of you and how you're the one to bring all these people together and create the community, and more importantly, how they were able to accomplish their goal within it. A goal, they will note, they didn't get done on their own in the first place!

If you think about it, even as far back as school, we've always wanted to be accepted. We've always wanted to be part of a group. That's why the nerdy kids stuck together at school, the popular kids stuck together at school, the Goth kids (along with their black eyeliner!) stuck together at school. It's that sense of community and that sense of belonging that everybody wants.

In reality, the community challenge helps you keep the needle moving. Every interaction that a person has with you drives them closer to achieving their goals. This becomes essential to your brand, your reputation, your teachings, and your business.

Think about what we're doing here. If they've taken each step with you, throughout this process so far, it's probably looked something like the following:

- They visited your website.
- They opted in and got your magnet.
- You've qualified them with your "next step" product.
- You've helped them achieve another goal as part of the challenge.

- You've introduced them to the power of community (something that'll come in very handy later on in your own Youpreneur journey).
- You've shown them how YOU can be the leader they need to make a difference in what they're chasing down themselves.

It's this buy-in that will consistently place you front of mind whenever anyone in your community thinks of a problem they're experiencing. You'll be seen as the hero they need to take them from one place in their own journey to the next.

You've become the go-to source in your industry for this group of people. You've become the leader that they need to move forward.

And that's exactly what we're going to discuss next. Moving forward.

PART 3
MONETIZING

9

FIGURING OUT WHAT TO SELL

T'S game time, Youpreneurs. Monetization is all about figuring out the different ways you can make money from all the hard work you have put into building your brand and business.

So far, we've discussed building your brand, how to launch it into the world, and then spreading your wings through marketing. If you've followed through, you are now TRULY on your way to setting yourself up as the authority and getting your business talked about on a more regular basis. As this happens, you'll be seen as an influencer, as a thought leader, and as the go-to expert in your industry.

As great as that sounds, however, it's all just a fun hobby unless *A) you can help people further*, and *B) you can actually make money doing it.*

No matter what field you are in, your strategy behind monetization is the key to any successful business. You have to figure out what you can sell and how you can get people to pay you for it. I want to say something right out of the gate of this chapter, which is probably one of the most important things you will get out of this whole book.

Charge What You're Worth, and Don't Apologize

The biggest mistake I see people make is they don't value their experience, the content they provide, and what they can do for people. Uncle Chris is telling you to charge what you're worth and don't ever say you are sorry for it.

If you've been waiting for permission to raise your prices for any of your existing products or services, then this is it. You've got permission. DO IT!

Before you can decide how to price your offerings, though, you have to first figure out what to actually sell. Communication is key here. To be able to figure out what you're going to sell to your audience, you need to talk to them. Chances are at this point you've already had a lot of conversations with people in your community. Through those conversations you can glean information that will lead you to an understanding of what they need and what you can offer them to continue to help them on their journey.

If you're not already having those conversations with your audience, then start right now. Make notes of exactly what people say to you. You can use a notebook, a text file on your computer, or even a note on your phone—whatever is the best way for you to gather that information so you can easily find it later.

If I'm having a great conversation with somebody at a conference, and I don't necessarily want to whip out my notebook right there and then, I might excuse myself and let them know

I need to reply to a text from my wife, and I'll just type something out on my phone so I don't forget. Maybe I'm getting old, but I have to write everything down—otherwise, chances are I will forget.

Setting yourself up with a *primary profit mentality*, which will allow you to pay yourself first, is key when it comes to not only *thinking* about making money, but also putting steps in place to be able to *actually* make money. The reality is you're not going to be able to launch a product or a service that's worth thousands and thousands of dollars right out of the gate. Your tribe probably isn't ready for that yet.

The bottom line is you want to get as much intel as you can gather so you know exactly what people want. That takes away the guessing game and allows you to go straight to higher-value content creation. That's the secret to figuring out what to sell. So, make a note of every idea that comes your way.

This goes back to when you first started building your online home. When you start out, you create content that you *think* people might need and want. Further down the line, it will become quite apparent what they *actually* need and want because they'll start telling you. This is just Communication 101. People want to be heard. If they're following you, it's because they think that you can bring value their way.

That same kind of communication is just as important when you actually start selling to them.

Nobody likes being sold to, but we love to buy!

It really just comes down to the way you sell. You don't want to always give the hard sell.

I've been in the sales business my entire career, and one of the biggest hang-ups I used to see when I would perform sales training for clients was that they were always worried about "the close." *I've got to focus on my close. I've got to practice my closing technique.* The fact of the matter is, if you've done everything else in the sales process correctly—you've prospected, you've qualified, you've built rapport, you've gained trust, you've handled the pitch well, you've gotten over the first bunch of objections, and you've handled more objections—if you've done all that right, the close will happen by itself.

It's just the natural conclusion to the sales process.

The same can be said for the process of monetizing your brand and your business online. If you've done all the steps in the process online, they'll buy what you're putting out. They might not even read the emails you send them, they'll just click the link, go to the website, and hit the *buy now* button. You might not need to spend all this time, effort, and money creating a beautiful website because you've been serving your audience, you've been listening to them, you've been communicating with them for a long time, and it's now time for that to pay off.

And while we're on the subject of things paying off, don't go soft on me here. Not only do people greatly underprice

Nobody likes **being sold to**, but we **love to buy!**

themselves, they also greatly underappreciate how brilliant they are at what they do for others. You deserve to be paid.

So how do you get that kind of communication started with your audience? I'm glad you asked! Remember this—it's simply conversation. Don't make this harder than it seems. The people in your audience, whether they're on your email list, following you on Facebook, or tweeting with you on Twitter, they are there because they are interested in what you are saying. So start a conversation and ask them what they would like to see from you.

If You Never Ask, You'll Never Know

The easiest way to find out what your audience is looking for is to simply ask them—by surveying them. You want to make it as easy as possible for your community to get involved in the survey. On your end, you need to be a little rigid: you want to be quite fundamental in what you're putting together and acutely aware of what you want to get out of this process.

Having that primary profit mentality and the kind of flexibility that comes with it gives you the ability to pivot on your ideas and change them when necessary to create an easy buying process for your customers.

When you're surveying your audience, keeping it really, really simple is the way to go.

Think about it like this: even though you've helped them a lot, and even if you have been working with them on and off for a while, your audience actually doesn't owe you anything at all. If they are completing your survey at this point, you should be very, very grateful. Keeping this process short and simple by making the questions easy to answer will allow you to get real feedback from your community survey.

I survey my audience once a year with no more than 10 questions. I use a service called SurveyMonkey. They have a free version if you're just starting out, but there is a paid version available that is 100 percent brandable, so you can add things like your logo to it.

Keep your survey simple by using a combination of multiple-choice options and some open-ended questions. This combo is important because when somebody answers an open-ended question, they give you information, and that is information you can act upon to put together the best product for them.

Surveying your audience is absolutely essential, but you've also got to understand how important it is not to bombard them with these surveys. As mentioned, I only survey my audience once a year, but you could decide to do it twice a year. I know some people do it more than that, but I personally feel like that's asking a lot from your audience.

If you're in the business industry, most people will be following you to learn how to make money in some way. If this is the case, the one thing to remember is you have to be focused on how you're going to make money for the individual members of your audience. The point of the survey is not only finding out what your audience wants and needs, but also how you can turn whatever it is that you end up providing into money for them.

If you can somehow suggest that by answering the survey you're going to help them ultimately make money, they're more likely to complete it. The encompassing goal here is to get the feedback you need to be able to actually create products, books, services, and experiences that your audience can obtain and use, in order to grow in whatever area they need growth in.

As a little inspiration for you, here are few sample questions from my last survey:

1. Of all the content that I produce, which way do you prefer to consume my training?
a) Blog Posts
b) Podcast Episodes
c) Online Videos
d) Infographics

2. What area of your business do you need the most help on currently?
a) Building
b) Marketing
c) Monetizing

3. If there was ONE piece of content that I could produce for you that would solve your biggest problem, what would it be and why?

That last question is an open-ended one. Meaning I'm going to get information out of the answers that'll help me in deciding which products and services to produce for my audience.

The bottom line is... survey your audience. Do it properly, do it professionally, and make it short and sweet.

The Power of On-the-Spot Conversations

Starting on-the-spot conversations with your audience—and I mean in person—is another great way to find out what they need help with, prior to going all-in on a product idea.

For me, this is the easiest and most personal way to be able to get feedback. I find these conversations not only useful during the pre-launch of products and services, but helpful after the launch as well. If someone didn't buy the product, I want to know why. I may ask questions like, *Hey, Mike... My recent productivity course . . . why didn't you buy it? What kept you from whipping out your credit card? Was it because it wasn't going to help you move forward? Was it because the messaging behind the pitch of the product or service was wrong for you?* If I know what didn't work, I can then go back and fix it before I offer the product or service again.

In-person conversations are real. People are more likely to be upfront and honest when you're sitting right in front of them. That's why I love short, sweet, to-the-point conversations. Talk to your audience whenever you have the opportunity (live events are particularly ripe for this). Get the "what are you struggling with" out of them. And here's a tip: Once they've divulged the goods, and I know what they are looking for or what they need, I like to close the conversation by asking them to take a quick selfie with me. Why do I do that? Because I want to say thank you to them for taking the time to talk with me and answer my questions.

By simply taking out my iPhone, shooting a quick selfie with them, tweeting that photo out to my audience, and tagging them in that tweet, I am letting that person know I appreciate the time they spent with me. Let me tell you, that is great P2P, right there. It's huge, and people love it.

In-person talk is best, but sometimes I have these conversations via Skype as well. I like to just reach out to random members in my community, particularly if they're vocal. I'll let them know I've got a couple of things I want to run by them that I would like their thoughts about and ask for them to hop on a 15-minute Skype conversation with me. I let them know I'd really value their opinion. They never say no. They're my clients or community members, so of course they will want to have a quick conversation with me.

Toward the end of the call, I always make sure to ask them if there's anything they're struggling with right now that I can help them with, and give them five minutes of free coaching. I get the feedback I want, and they get a few minutes of my time without having to pay for it. Everybody's happy.

Getting Social to Dig Deeper

Social media is another avenue for having conversations with your audience to help you figure out what it is they are looking for. The point of social media is to converse with people and share ideas back and forth in a safe and casual style. As a business owner, you want as much engagement as possible through your social networks.

Learn to enjoy quick conversations, publicly and privately, to gauge what your audience is looking for.

Here are a few strategies that I employ on a regular basis to get feedback and kick off conversations with the people I want to eventually do business with.

The Sniper Tweet Strategy

I have sniper tweeting moments when I'll strategically send a person a tweet and start a conversation. I like to keep an eye on hashtags that I've created and see who is sharing or retweeting that hashtag. Say I notice that someone has been really active in tweeting out some of my blog posts or my podcast content. When I see that happening, I'll send that person a quick direct tweet, or even a public tweet saying thank you and start a conversation with them. Ultimately, that conversation will lead to me asking them what they like most about whatever it was they shared and how I can elaborate on that for future product ideas.

I call them sniper tweets because they are targeted. I am specifically sending them to people who are engaging in my

Learn to enjoy quick conversations, **publicly and privately**, to gauge what your audience is looking for.

content already and who liked what they saw enough to share it. These people are primed and ready to give me feedback on the spot. It's a powerful tool for sure.

The "Personal" Video Strategy

The power of a personalized video is incredible—personal direct video messages can be used for reaching out and surveying your audience. You can send a direct video message on almost any social media platform now. It's fast and it's easy, but very effective. All you need to do is turn your phone around, look into the camera and say, *Hey, Christine. I just wanted to say thanks for checking out that blog post on how to become more productive. I appreciate your retweeting it. Let me ask you, what was the biggest takeaway for you and what did that takeaway solve for you?*

Just that one quick video message to them can really make an impact.

First of all, they won't expect it. It will really catch them off guard and surprise them that you would take the time to acknowledge them for mentioning you or your content. It also opens the door for a back and forth to get a little bit more information about how you can continue to help them.

The Facebook Messaging Strategy

Quite regularly, I'll reach out to people on Facebook. I like to do this particularly around my events. I may ask to find out what people want to get out of my upcoming live event, or I may want to know what they thought about the event we just finished up. It's a great way to get instant input from your most targeted audience, your paying customers.

Messaging is not something that has to take a lot of time either. Sometimes, I do it myself and sometimes one of my virtual assistants will help me out. We'll fire off some quick messages to people, reaching out to them privately, off the public grid, and find out exactly what they would like to see me create for them in the future.

Getting that feedback from your customers and prospective customers is huge. It allows you to lay the foundation of your monetization strategy.

If you can't figure out what to sell, you won't be able to build something to sell.

Don't be shy, talk to your audience, find out what they want, and build the solutions they are looking for. If you don't engage with your community on a regular basis by emailing them, you'll be forgotten by them. They'll move on and start learning

If you can't **figure out what to sell**, you won't be able to **build something to sell**.

from somebody else who will become their new favorite, and you don't want that to happen.

Email really is where the party's at when it comes to this side of your business, which is why I put such a focus on continually growing and pruning my own email list. I'm letting you know right here and now—if you are on my email list (or get on it soon!), you will get an email from me every single week. In that email, I will have links to the new content that I've published over that last week, as well as any live events, promotions, and personal updates too.

It will take you no more than one minute to read that email. They're short, sweet, and to the point. As a Youpreneur, if you pay very close attention, you'll find that it's the same people who open up your emails every week. Week in, week out.

If you've put this chapter's plan into practice, it's *these people* who probably told you what to sell in those conversations you were having, and now, they are the ones who are going to end up buying what you put out to the world!

Socrates nailed it—the best way to please any people or group is to find out what they want and then give it to them.

CASE STUDY

NAME: Anissa Holmes
BUSINESS NAME: Delivering WOW
WEBSITE: DeliveringWow.com

Background

Anissa Holmes has been a dentist for 18 years . . . and she has built several start-up practices. The struggle for her was creating balance between seeing patients and having the freedom to take herself away to spend time with her family or to travel. She committed to a two-year plan to create a practice that could run without her—she hired a coach, learned everything she could about running a business, and in two years, she tripled revenue and was debt free. When faced with the question "what's next?" she decided to write a book to share her story with other dentists of how she was able to achieve her goals.

It became obvious to her that no one knew who she was yet, so she started a podcast, and began to build her brand online.

Establishing Authority

The first thing Anissa did was she got in front of people. She started getting on other people's podcasts, she led a Facebook group, and she reached out to other influencers.

Anissa overdelivered on everything she did and she made sure she was showing up in a way that people saw her being real and authentic. When you overdeliver, your customers will be your raving fans and they are happy to provide testimonials to help you continue to grow and scale.

Three Things to Grow Business Effectively

1. Anissa says an ABUNDANCE mindset is of the utmost importance. Reaching out to others who serve your industry in a different capacity and helping to grow their businesses by exposing them to your tribe is extremely important. If you do this, those people will reciprocate.

   Look at just one example of this from Anissa: "I teach Facebook, and I did an educational workshop/webinar for Fred Joyal of 1-800-DENTISTS. This was to add value to his 700 registrants. They definitely got value, and this one webinar put me in front of so many who otherwise would not have known about me. I can track thousands of dollars of revenue that came from that webinar alone."

2. Starting a podcast: Hosting a podcast has allowed Anissa to have her voice where she can add value and help people for free, which then puts them on a path of ascension to her paid programs. It's also allowed her to quickly connect with industry influencers who would like to use her platform to get their message out there.

3. Creating a VALUE-packed Facebook group and encouraging other influencers in her industry to be a part and share. In her Facebook group, people can get to know the real Anissa and how she serves. Having other experts in the group has allowed for rich content for the members of the group as well as having the ability for the other influencers to bring their tribe to the group and learn about Anissa and all she offers.

Most Profitable Monetization

Anissa believes that having a well-defined ascension plan for everyone who finds her is crucial for her success. People start with reading her blogs, listening to her podcast, and getting value from her groups. From there they join her membership site (Delivering WOW U), and for $97 a month they get access to profit-generating business trainings and a monthly group coaching call. Then they can join her $697 Facebook Boot Camp or her $3,000 Business Acceleration Boot Camps. The next level from there is her $20,000 Inner Circle.

Here's what Anissa had to say about being a YOUPRENEUR:

Chris and the Youpreneur Community have been with me from day one of my online journey. When I joined, I didn't even know what a funnel was! As a member of the community, Chris gave me direct feedback on my initial website and even helped me to come up with the subtitle for my book. Other members who were already podcasting gave tons of feedback and support, and in a Youpreneur Mastermind, my first online course was formed. I've also met some incredible people along my journey who are also members. One of these people was Mike Morrison, who I met at a London Mastermind. He shared with me the value of creating membership sites. Prior to meeting him, I didn't know of such a thing.

The members are people who share and are all there to lift each other up. This I know comes from the tribe that Chris wanted to create, because he's a person who truly cares. Youpreneur is the way Chris is creating his legacy.

I have made over a half million dollars in my first year in my online journey. But what's more important than the money is that I am now creating and helping others to create their legacies as well.

10

BUILDING YOUR OWN YOUPRENEUR ECOSYSTEM

W HEN I first started planning the Youpreneur Mastermind Community, one of the big things I knew I was going to have to teach people to do was to build out their own Youpreneur ecosystem.

Actually, I've touched on just about all of that ecosystem already. It consists of your offerings—coaching, software, courses, live events, books, training, services, products, and all the rest of it. *That* is your ecosystem. Now we have to figure out how it all works for you.

Here's the thing: I can't teach you how or what will work. Each Youpreneur ecosystem is unique. The fact is, your ecosystem is a self-stimulating, always evolving, and pivoting environment. It's based entirely on what you can do and what your community and customers need you to do. It's never the same for any two people, it's always different, and it's always changing. That's actually what makes it hard to teach, because there's no simple plug-and-play program to make it work. That's also what makes it so bloody exciting to get involved with, because you will never get bored with it.

Your ecosystem must be based on your strengths and your audience's needs and wants. As you build it out, be careful that you're not putting all of your eggs in one monetization basket. That is never a good idea. You want to make sure that you're diversifying income streams as much as possible. The ideal plan is to have several flows of income as a Youpreneur, and each one of those should be designed to help people by offering your expertise in a deep, value-oriented way.

One of the first steps in properly building out a Youpreneur ecosystem, which will fundamentally make your business future-proof, is to figure out how you want to monetize your expertise.

Let's face it, monetization is the life force of any business. If you aren't making money, you're not going to be in business for very long. As a Youpreneur, you have a lot of monetization weapons to choose from. Knowing the benefits of each and when to use them is paramount.

So, let's start breaking these options down and, as a result, building that ecosystem up.

Why You Must Be Seen to Sell

Before I go into monetization methods and discuss them one by one, I want to talk about why you must be seen to sell to be regarded as an influencer in the first place.

The fact is, there are a lot of different ways to build up recognition. I've covered many of these already, right here in the book, with the most special and influential being the creation of helpful content. Solving people's problems via your content and marketing that content so that it's easily found, consumed, and shared (with more people you can affect positively) should always be at the center of everything that you do as a Youpreneur.

However, in our quest to blow people's minds with how amazing our blog, podcast, videos, and live streams are, we have to first address a few points that are crucial to building the ecosystems our businesses are going to need to remain profitable and memorable.

The Freebie "Influencer" Never Wins

Giving away content and solving people's problems for free can go a long way toward raising awareness about you and your business, and it certainly makes you approachable to prospects interested in building a relationship. Eventually, though, there will come a time when you have to put some kind of monetary amount next to what you are doing to solve your audience's bigger problems. Putting a dollar sign, or a pound sign, or a euro sign—whatever tickles your fancy—on your knowledge and experience moves you out of the freebie influencer sphere and into the realm of expert. There's a very fine line between being known as a freebie content producer and as a real true-blue entrepreneurial influencer.

The difference is just making a very clear decision to say, "I'm going to charge for this one." It's as simple as that.

Freebie influencers will never win in the long run because they wait too long to make the transition from free to monetized content. After a certain amount of time receiving free content, particularly if it's very high quality, an audience will become programmed to think that everything they're going to get, every solution offered them, will be free of charge. When a freebie influencer eventually comes out with a course, product, or service with any kind of monetary value to it, chances are their market has become so used to not spending money with them, they simply just won't buy.

It's very important to understand the power of being seen to sell on a regular basis—that way there's no surprise. Your market will be used to you offering different types of value at a cost and will have no problem with opening up their wallets and giving you their credit card—as long as it solves a problem for them, obviously.

The Value of a Dollar/Pound/Euro

My father used to say, "If you look after the pennies, the pounds will look after themselves." It's so very true. Making a monetary investment instantly increases the stakes for the buyer to actually take action on whatever they've purchased. You're not going to buy an iPhone or an iPad and not use it, are you? Because of the investment you made, you're going to use the product. The same can be said for online courses, products, and services that we get from the people we know, love, and trust. As a Youpreneur, you want your audience to appreciate that there is true value behind a monetary investment.

People Will Pay for Access

The bottom line here, in regards to being seen as a leader who sells, is to understand that people nowadays are more likely to pay for access to you, your experience, and your wisdom than ever before.

If you understand the value of a dollar and know that people will pay to have access to you as an industry go-to leader, then it becomes easy to see how you can offer your content for a great fee. Eventually, you will want to cross over from being just useful to having people pulling out their wallets to gain access to your higher-priced offerings.

Getting them to give you money is the difference between having a successful blog or podcast and having a successful business that *utilizes* blogging and podcasting.

Before you even figure out the monetization strategy or strategies you're going to implement, you have to appreciate and respect the system of the sales process. Because eventually, you will have to start making money out of all of this. (Have I said this before?) Otherwise, what you're doing is just pursuing a hobby, and you probably don't need another hobby.

One of my favorite pastimes is to build LEGO sets with my children (oh, okay, sometimes I build them on my own too!). But, as much as I love LEGO, it isn't going to pay the bills, is it?

Introducing Your Starting Five

I'm one of the rare Englishmen who has very little interest in football. Instead, I'm a huge basketball fan (Boston Celtics fan for life!), and so I use the basketball analogy of the "Starting Five" (the first five players on the court at the beginning of the game) whenever I work with anyone on the beginning of their monetization strategy.

I don't like to think short-term when it comes to monetization in any business. Instead, I think medium- to long-term. Obviously, you've got to start somewhere, so short-term thinking is okay—but only to get the ball rolling. I like to plan out for a period of about 12 months. This 12-month monetization strategy that you'll be using is based around utilizing the aforementioned Starting Five.

These are the five things you can plan out and implement the fastest to get your business profitable and moving in the right direction.

Now, I want to make something very clear: I'm not saying you need to implement all of these strategies and have them running for the next 12 months. However, what I am saying is that some of these you will act on immediately, and some of them you will start planning to use more toward the end of that period. In other words, start slow and build to the point that, within the next 12 months, you will have all five of these monetization strategies in place and active in your business.

You're not going to move the needle on all of them at one time. Slow and steady wins the race when it comes to building a profitable Youpreneur ecosystem. You need to have a mindset that is focused on where you want to take your ecosystem in the second, the third, the fourth, the fifth year, and so on and so on.

What's important is that you hit the ground running, and you do that by grabbing the lowest-hanging fruit, plain and simple.

1. Coaching and Consulting

For experts, coaching is the absolute lowest-hanging monetization fruit there is.

I touched on how to start out when I talked earlier about expanding your reach, being seen, and implementing more expert-positioning strategies by building your coaching page.

Coaching may not be for everyone over the long haul, but it is definitely something that everybody should try out when they are just getting started. Really it comes down to that one all-important question, the question that I've talked about a few times already throughout the course of our time together: what is the one big problem that you're solving for your customer?

The answer to that is the issue you should coach people on. You might get to the point where you coach on two or three problems. A lot of life coaches do this. They might help people get over divorce or get over a loss, or they may do both.

Making coaching your first monetization strategy is as simple as figuring out what problem you're going to solve, putting up a great-looking coaching page on your website, deciding what you're going to charge on either an hourly basis or a recurring monthly setup, and then hitting the publish button. Start to promote it, and you are on your way.

Just recently, a very active Youpreneur Community member reached out to me, saying he needed to raise some additional funds quickly. He was planning a holiday and wanted a little more pocket money while he was away with his wife.

For experts, **coaching is the absolute lowest-hanging monetization fruit** there is.

I said to him, "Well, the next time you send an email to your list, add a P.S. at the bottom of that email and say, 'I've just opened up three one-hour coaching sessions on my calendar in the next two weeks—You pick my brain on anything you think I can help you with for an entire hour for just $1,000. If you're interested, go ahead and hit reply, and we can set things up!'" He sold all three spots just hours after sending out that email. Funny enough, he now actually does it quite regularly.

It just goes to show you, people will pay for access to you and your experience, but you've got to tell them you're actually offering it. People are happy to pay for knowledge they don't have.

2. Affiliate Marketing

Affiliate marketing is a great way to start monetizing your brand. It's been an active way to monetize a website almost as long as advertisement and sponsorship. Basically, you put a link on your website that sends your visitor to an offer, and if they buy, you make a commission on the sale.

What I love about affiliate marketing is it's short-term, but it could be used for medium- and long-term profitability as well. As an influencer, you've built up an audience through your email list, blog readers, and podcast listeners. That means you have an active market that other influencers would love to get in front of.

Let's say there is a piece of software you use and are in love with. This product makes your life so much easier, you couldn't live without it. Go ahead and say to your audience, "This software will help you, too, because I know you're struggling with the same issue." You create an introduction to that piece of software, and any time someone buys it through your link, you get a commission from the sale.

If you want to see affiliate marketing in action, just visit my personal resources page on my blog: ChrisDucker.com/ Resources—there are several affiliate links on that page.

The cool thing here is not only can you promote affiliate products on a short-term basis, you can put those links into your email auto-responder and promote them on an ongoing, automated basis. When somebody signs up for your opt-in magnet, they end up getting a series of emails, and one of those emails could promote this product or service.

Now here's a warning for you. Just because you can pretty much pitch any product or service to the engaged audience you've built doesn't mean you should. As a general rule of thumb, I always say do not promote anything as an affiliate you are not personally involved with in some way, shape, or form. Whether that involvement is as a joint-venture partner or just as a customer, it doesn't matter. You should not pitch something to your audience that you are not directly connected with and/or utilizing yourself.

I get probably two or three emails a week from people who want me to pitch their course, product, or software to my engaged audience. If I don't know them from Adam, or I don't use their service, I just won't do it—plain and simple.

If you can't stand behind a product, then you shouldn't promote it!

With that said, affiliate marketing truly is a short-, medium-, and long-term strategy. It's low-hanging fruit, very easy to set up, and a great way to be able to make money over time.

3. Online Courses

The next monetization strategy is online courses or any kind of info product. In reality, you've already been creating this type of content in short form: your e-books, your coaching videos,

If you can't **stand behind** a product, then you shouldn't **promote it!**

or maybe the audio downloads that you've provided to your audience for free. What you're going to do now is take this content up several notches. Instead of having, say, three 10-minute videos for a total of 30 minutes of training that you give away, you'll now expand those solutions into an entire course of content that you'll sell.

One way to approach developing a course is to break down solving a bigger problem into a series of smaller solutions that you can guide your community through step-by-step. You can create video, audio, or written content, or combine them to deliver one well-organized course.

The first thing I would do is figure out what sections I want to cover in that course. Then I'd figure out how many modules I need and how many lessons will be in each module. Next I'd go ahead and start creating video, audio, or written content, or maybe a combination of all of it. Then I'll put all of that into one well-organized course.

Once it's all put together, place the course on your website, or upload it somewhere for people to consume, and then market it and start making sales. This is a medium- to long-term strategy. You can make money as soon as you launch the course, and you can make money by continuing to promote it for years to come.

> To get a free Process Blueprint on How to Create and Sell a Digital Product, just visit **Youpreneur.com/ ReadersOnly** for instant access.

The beautiful thing about courses is that you can build up to having a whole library of them. If your field of expertise is in personal productivity, for example, you could start off by producing a course on productivity strategies for business owners. You could then put together a course on productivity for parents. After that, a course on productivity for authors, then marketers, then teachers, and so on.

Online courses are gold. They are a monetization strategy that can really help move the needle up for you and help you continue to build your influence as well.

4. Membership Sites

Okay, let's move on to a really long-term strategy. I'll be honest, I ignored this one for the longest time. In fact, I purposely tried to stay away from creating a membership site because it's about as unpassive in terms of generating income as you can get.

When you build a membership site, you're basically building a product that sits online, and people pay to have access to it. Maybe you charge a monthly fee, maybe it's quarterly, maybe it's annually. Whatever the fee schedule, people pay on a regular basis to continue to have access to whatever material or services you're providing. Membership sites, like the Youpreneur Community, are deemed the holy grail of online business. However, they're not for everyone because they are an ongoing service-based business model, which is one of the reasons it took me a while to get on board with them.

As you can plainly tell, I've changed my stance on membership sites—I love them now! The Youpreneur Community was set up in September of 2015, after I'd been planning it for over a year. I took my time because I knew once it was out there in the world, there was no going back.

You can't "set and forget" a membership business. You've got to show up all the time. I'll tell you right now, you shouldn't even consider starting a membership unless you are genuinely ready to show up routinely. You also have to understand this is not going to necessarily make a quick profit. Membership sites actually take a lot of time to grow.

You should only launch a membership if you're all about leveraging your authority on an ongoing basis, if you want to take your customer loyalty to the next level, and if the idea of recurring and predictive income is attractive to you.

The membership model is the poster child of recurring and predictive income!

My tune changed on membership sites when I finally figured out the importance of predictable income as an online business owner. I'd had this kind of income for over 10 years as a bricks-and-mortar entrepreneur, but it took me a long time to figure out its importance as someone doing business on the Internet.

It helps set a strong foundation for your business when each and every month you know roughly where you're going to be in regards to your income, before that month even starts. If you want to make a little more money, you put more cash behind your marketing and you bring more members in. Your vibe will attract your tribe, and you want to get your tribe into your membership as quickly as possible.

So how much content should you put on a membership site? Well that's a very good question, because it's different for everybody. Some memberships out there have very little content in them. They might publish one workshop a month, then the rest of what people are paying for is, quite frankly, access to the influencer who's running the membership or access to other members inside a private forum.

Rant Alert: On the subject of private forums and discussion boards, I see way too many people utilizing a Facebook group for their paid membership site. You cannot and should not do this, because you are building your house on rented land.

The membership model is the **poster child** of **recurring and predictive income!**

We all know that Facebook loves to move the goal posts. They make a lot of changes all the time. It's part of their mission to keep things evolving, to keep things changing and updated. I get it from a business perspective for Facebook. For us, however, if you're building a paid community on a Facebook group, what happens tomorrow if Facebook decides to dump the "groups" idea completely? You will lose everything. Please don't do this. Make sure if you're going to have a discussion forum component in your membership that you build it out on your own server.

Back to how much content you need in a membership. It really depends on what you want to do and what you feel your audience needs and wants from you. A sample month of content might look something like this:

- **Week #1:** You might have a mini-course of three or four videos.

- **Week #2:** You might have a checklist of some variety or a swipe file.

- **Week #3:** You might have a live mastermind call.

- **Week #4:** You might have some kind of additional membership perks you can pass on or an additional piece of content you created for members.

Ultimately, though, it really depends on you, what you want to deliver, what your audience likes and needs, and how much work you actually want to put into it.

Pricing also comes into play when determining the amount of content you offer. If your membership price is $30 a month, people are going to expect a lot less from you than if it is $100 a month.

Membership sites are not for everyone. If you are looking for passive income, look elsewhere, but if you are looking for recurring income, membership sites are where it's at! I now love them because they are predictive, and they truly are one of the best ways to serve your tribe in a very deep way. I've got to be honest with you—of all the things I've done in my 14 years as an entrepreneur, building the Youpreneur Community is the best decision I've ever made. I've been able to put everything that I want to do to help people in my niche into an easily consumable format and offer members a true community at the same time. And as an added bonus, I've actually become pretty good friends with a lot of my paying customers.

The membership site strategy went from the one thing I avoided like the plague to the very best thing I've ever done. You're not going to come out of the gate with this straightaway when you begin to monetize, but you certainly want to look at this model a little further down the line, as you focus in on building your Youpreneur ecosystem.

For more information on membership sites, I strongly suggest you check out this podcast episode with the man I call the "Godfather of Memberships," Mike Morrison: ChrisDucker .com/Episode182.

5. Live Events

I've held the last spot in the Starting Five lineup for live events. These are a big plus to any Youpreneur ecosystem. Live events have been a game changer for me—not only attending them, but actually holding them myself. I started out offering live mastermind and workshop events, then ran my Tropical Think Tank in the Philippines for four years. I now have the Youpreneur Summit, which takes place in London every year. Being able to get people together in person to learn together, laugh together, brainstorm together, and break bread together is extremely powerful. Live events really take you to the next level.

Live events are not easy to organize, especially when they hit a certain scale, but the good news is you can start small and build up size over a period of time. My first ever live event was in late 2010. I had only 11 people attend. We sat around a table and just spent the day brainstorming with each other. That was it—that was the event.

Fast forward, and I'm now putting on live events with hundreds and hundreds of people in attendance. Don't go too big too early, but work your way up. It's worth the effort. Live events just put everything you're doing into a completely different stratosphere, because what do people do when they're at live events? They talk about it. They take pictures, they tweet, they mention it on Facebook and on other social media channels, and that just gives you a beautiful and viral marketing effect every single time you hold one.

I'll never stop doing live events because people will pay to learn from the best—especially in a live setting. But more importantly, these events are quite simply too much fun to stop. I just love the buzz of bringing "my people" together to build relationships, forge plans, and ultimately have a great time!

Two Other Important Monetization Strategies

While my Starting Five are favorite monetization strategies for me, let's talk really quick about a few other options. And we'll start with the very thing you're holding in your hands right now (or listening to, if you went the audiobook route!).

Books.

Your $20 Business Card

Books are huge from a monetization perspective. Not only will a book become the best twenty-dollar business card you'll ever print, but it will also help position you as an influencer at exactly the same time. Books are flexible too. You don't have to just do a physical book; you can do audio and e-book formats too.

Most people think writing a book means they have to follow the old-school traditional publishing rules. Before you can get a traditional publishing deal, you have to put together a proposal, sample chapters, and all kinds of other stuff, then wait for a gatekeeper's approval before you're even allowed to get started.

However, as a Youpreneur, you can self-publish your first book. You don't need to worry about a traditional publishing agreement.

Hal Elrod is a very good friend. He self-published *The Miracle Morning* and has sold hundreds of thousands of copies. And, because he self-published the book, he's getting the lion's share of the profit with every copy sold.

If you've not written a book before, or if you have and you want to add another into the mix, here are a few tips to help you get started:

1. Define your audience. As with any endeavor you pursue as a Youpreneur, you must begin by identifying your audience. Who are you writing for? Why do they need your book?

2. Define your purpose. Why are you writing a book? Sounds like an obvious question, but I assure you it's not. You must know the purpose behind your book and the effort of writing it before you begin.

3. Draft an outline. An outline is basically your future book's table of contents, with a few bullet points under each "chapter heading" to help you make sense of how your book is

unfolding from beginning to end. It's a great way to get a bird's eye view of your book.

4. Turn those bullet points into sentences and paragraphs. This is the step where you essentially trick yourself into writing the book. Well, almost!

5. Get a fresh perspective. Whether you hire an editor or engage a few beta readers from your network or community, you absolutely must get a fresh pair of eyes on your book before you publish. It's invaluable.

Professional Services

Offering services to your clients generates another great income opportunity. This might not be for everyone, but adding a service to what you offer may be something you want to look at in the future.

For example, I became the go-to guy in the virtual assistance and outsourcing industry online. As a result, I have a company called Virtual Staff Finder, which helps busy entrepreneurs find high-quality, experienced virtual assistants in the Philippines to help run, support, and grow their businesses.

The service was already set up when my first book, *Virtual Freedom*, came out in early 2014. However, because of that book and all the people reading it and saying to themselves, "Well, I need a VA now!" we doubled the size of the team in a year and continue to be a very profitable service-based company—one that sits squarely in my own Youpreneur ecosystem, as you'll see below.

Clearly there are lots of different ways you can monetize your influence, but you have to start somewhere. Don't get hung up on trying to do everything, and remember that what someone else does may not be right for your audience.

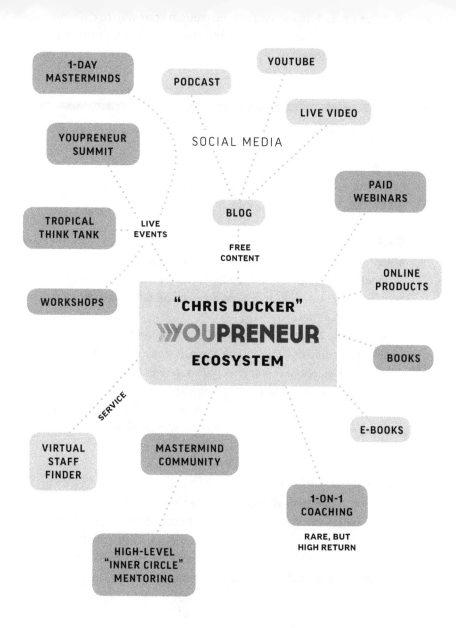

Start small and grow.

Get the monetization ball rolling by working through my Starting Five first, and you will be well on your way to cashing in on your experience and setting things up for a profitable, long-term business.

CASE STUDY

NAME: Mike Morrison & Callie Willows
BUSINESS NAME: The Membership Guys
WEBSITE: TheMembershipGuys.com

Background

Mike Morrison and Callie Willows originally ran a digital marketing agency. Through that company, they were directly involved in countless successful membership websites, e-learning sites, and online communities.

Eventually Mike and Callie knew they wanted to help more people than could realistically hire them, so they started blogging and podcasting about membership sites, and then of course they opened up their very own membership program.

Today, they no longer take on clients or do any coaching or consultancy—the entirety of their business is 100 percent focused on helping people inside their membership.

Establishing Authority

Mike and Callie believe that going "all in" on their niche and remaining steadfast in their focus on that audience has helped them most when establishing their authority. They could have quite easily strayed into producing content about things like online courses, other subscription models, or general online business, but the consistency and depth they achieved by keeping that laser focus has been a huge part in their success.

Mike and Callie also found that podcasting was perhaps one of the most effective methods of quickly establishing their *voice* in a way that the written word simply can't compare with, and it remains one of their biggest sources of new members to this day.

Three Things to Grow Business Effectively

1. Segmenting their audience and producing content, lead magnets, and sales funnels that cater specifically to those segments has driven conversions right up compared to the early days when, like most people, they had a broader approach.

   This isn't something subtle that Mike and Callie do in the background either. As soon as you go to their website, they're channeling you into one of their core segments. This helps them refine their marketing message to make it far more targeted and, as a result, more likely to convert.

2. Recognizing that marketing doesn't end with the sale. Perfecting their customer experience has been as important, if not more so, than bringing in sales, particularly because their business depends on recurring revenue.

   Mike and Callie have great member onboarding and focus on delivering ongoing value to encourage people to not only stick around long-term but also to refer others and give positive testimonials and feedback they can then leverage in their marketing to really tap into social proof.

3. Mike and Callie embrace their roles as problem solvers. Every piece of content they create, whether it's a blog, podcast, Facebook Live video, or webinar, aims to solve a problem.

   They listen to the questions their audience has, their frustrations, challenges, goals, and problems, and as a result, have an endless source of inspiration for content ideas. They believe if they help people solve their small problems, those people will trust them to solve larger ones via a paid offering.

Most Profitable Monetization

Their membership site is the absolute core of Mike and Callie's business. Everything else is secondary. Through it, they've been able to completely move away from trading time for money and working one-on-one with clients, and as a result, their business has stable, predictable, recurring revenue that just keeps growing.

Here's what Mike and Callie had to say about being a
YOUPRENEUR:

That entrepreneurial loneliness that Chris so often talks about is absolutely real, no matter how successful you are. Being part of a community of like-minded business owners is incredibly valuable. Just knowing that you have people there to bounce ideas off of, get feedback from, or even when you can walk into an event and know a handful of people there already, it makes a huge difference.

11

DEVELOPING A STRONG PRICING STRATEGY

I N the last chapter, we talked about different monetization weapons you can use to actually make money from your expertise. Figuring out what you want to sell is step one of the monetization process, but steps two and three are just as important. Now it's time to talk about how to price your products and services (step two).

Checking Up on Competitors

When establishing price points, you have to start by checking up on your competitors. However, for Youpreneurs there's one quite strange yet obvious truth.

When you build The Business of You, there are no real competitors.

Here's the reasoning behind this statement. You're basing your business and marketing around you, your personality, your experience, and the people you want to help out and serve the most. Regardless of what industry or niche you're in, there are no real competitors out there competing to be you, because you are unique in every way and no one else could possibly be you better than you can. However, chances are there're certainly other people out there competing for the attention of the same market you're trying to attract, and doing it in a very similar fashion. This is the competition we're talking about in this chapter.

When you **build The Business of You**, there are **no real competitors.**

Let's say you're someone helping people create online courses, for example. You've got a lot of experience in the educational field, you've been involved with universities in the past, helping them create curriculums and things like that, and now you have developed your own side hustle and are working on building up your own profile as a course-creation ninja.

Here's the problem: there are other people out there already doing that.

In fact, actually, I'll go out on a limb and say that there are probably people out there doing exactly what you're doing in the same industry that you're doing it in right now. And they may have already been in that marketplace for quite some time. But they are not you; they don't have your experience or your personality.

As a Youpreneur, you want to keep a keen eye on what they are doing. You've got to look at what they are offering, how they're offering it, and what they are charging for access to those products or services. Obviously, you don't want to start copying them, but look at what's working for others so that you can develop your own ideas. You don't have to be the originator all the time. If there is a proven method or standard already in place, it's good to use that as a platform from which you launch your own efforts to a specific audience.

Don't be concerned with looking similar to other people in your niche. You have something none of them do.

The secret weapon for a Youpreneur is simply just being you all the time.

That's the differentiating factor. That's the MVP part of your business. You are the most valuable player when it comes to keeping yourself ahead of the competition. So look for people trying to attract the same audience that you are. Watch and see what they are doing. Follow their lead as to what to offer, how to offer it, and how much to charge. Then implement the secret weapon by adding your flare into the mix.

The **secret weapon** for a Youpreneur is simply just **being you all the time**.

Building a Pricing Structure

Once you know what others in the space are doing, you can figure out how you're going to build out your pricing options and structure on the products and the services you want to offer. These might include items from our Starting Five, such as coaching, online courses, a membership, and even tickets to a live event. Whatever you choose, you can now start to price your offerings in a way that shows the value of your expertise.

The overall focus when it comes to pricing is that you've got to charge what you're worth, and as I have said before, don't apologize for it. So many people just don't see the actual value they add and undercharge for their time as a coach or consultant, or undercharge for their courses. If you do this, you set a standard that you may not be able to recover from later.

I have been guilty of undercharging in the past. I've had friends, mentors, and coaches come to me and say, "Chris, what the hell are you doing? You are so undercutting your value here." Sometimes it can be difficult for you to see your own worth, but trust me, you are more significant than you think you are.

I use a specific technique to help me avoid undercharging for access to my expertise. I double my pricing. That's right, I will get the price point to where I think it needs to be, and then I will double it. That seems scary, I know, but when I do this, I sell more as a result of it.

> Want a free Process Blueprint showing you exactly how to Devise a Strong Pricing Strategy? Just visit **Youpreneur.com/ ReadersOnly** and get instant access.

Here's the thing to remember when you start setting your prices. You can start high and decrease it from there, if things don't work out. However, it's so much harder to start low and increase incrementally over time. People will feel like they're getting a raw deal. Charge what you're worth—it's the single most important thing you can do.

What are you doing when you become a Youpreneur? You are selling your expertise. You're selling your experience. People are going to pay for access to knowledge. Price your information accordingly and make sure you prove the value.

Testing Your Idea

Now that you have your products and services in mind, and you've set up your pricing structure, it's time to test your ideas. There are maybe four main ways to test your offerings.

The "Hit Reply Now" Test

This is a very easy and quick test to do. Basically you send an email to your subscribers, with the following:

Hi [First Name]:

I've listened to all my subscribers and I understand what you need help with the most. As a result I've decided to work tirelessly putting together this course/book/event for you.

It's going to cover [mention three to four main benefits/features]. When we're done covering these together, you will be [whatever the desired outcome is]. If this is something that you would be interested in, all you need to do is just one thing...

Hit "reply" right now and let me know!

Best,
Chris

Take the number of emails that were sent, and then compare that to the number of emails that were opened and replied to. If you sent a ton of emails and very few people responded, then you need to reinvestigate your offer. If you get a flood of responses, then you know the idea is a good one, and you should invest more marketing efforts into that particular offer.

The "Dry Test" Landing Page Test

I got the term *dry test* from the infomercial industry, which I was involved with many moons ago. You know the infomercials that are on at two o'clock in the morning? You grab your credit card, and you buy the thing that's made in China that you'll never use, but you were half-asleep at the time, and it just made perfect sense in the middle of the night—that kind of thing!

Dry testing is basically selling a product that you're not quite ready to fulfill. In the infomercial world, companies buy the airtime required to show the infomercial. People will be standing by to take your call and to help you place your order, but the orders won't actually be fulfilled live. All they're wanting to do at that moment is to see how many times the phone rings and how many people want to order.

Once they have their numbers, if they feel like the product is successful enough, they will go ahead and order inventory as well as ramp up the media buying time. That is why so often with infomercials you'll see shipping is 30 to 45 days out. The reason for the delay is they've actually got to buy the products, get them into inventory, and fulfill the orders within the time period.

When it comes to your online product, dry testing works on a similar principle. You will create a landing page that has all of the features and benefits of the product you are planning to produce on it. The site looks pretty and has your branding. You talk about how great your product or service is, and have a *buy now* button on there. That button tracks clicks, to gauge interest.

I suggest using a very simple WordPress plug-in called Pretty Link. Pretty Link will basically allow you to track how many times somebody clicks on a link. It's very easy to set up.

If desired, you can go one step further here, too, by having a pop-up box appear when someone clicks that *buy now* button, and have them insert their email to go on a waitlist for when the product is available.

By creating that landing page, you can figure out how many people will buy your product or order your service. You'll know within a specific period of time whether or not it's going to be worthwhile for you to build out that particular thing or not. You're basically saying, *this is what I intend to do, but I haven't actually finished it up yet.* You're dry testing the product idea itself. Once you get the numbers that make you happy, create the course and start to sell it.

The Facebook Ad Test

What I love about Facebook ads is that they're extremely targeted from a demographic perspective. You can zoom them way down to territories of countries, even to cities, if you want. You can pick male, female, or age groups. You can pick interests. This is an advertiser's dream and takes target marketing to a whole new level.

The other great thing about Facebook ads is they're reasonably priced. You have total control over your advertising budget. You can set a low daily budget, and when your ads have hit their spending limits, Facebook will turn them off for the rest of the day. This allows you to test different ads. By changing the titles and subtitles, imagery, color schemes, or wording you can see which ad pulls the best, or gets clicked on the most. Now you're able to test the ads you run, as well as the product offer you are making.

Full disclosure here: the title of this book was tested using Facebook ads. I think I started with six or seven different titles. I got it down to a leading three, and after that really went hard to actually nail it down. I think I wound up spending $500 or $600 to find the title of this book. It was all done via Facebook ads. I simply monitored the click-throughs. The advert with the title that got clicked on the most showed me which title I wanted to use.

The Ballsy "Presale" Test

Next, you've got what I call the ballsy presale test. This is actually just taking the dry test landing page strategy one step further. You have your landing page, you've still got your *buy now* button, but instead of just tracking the clicks on that link (or having someone opt in to a waitlist), when someone hits the *buy now* button, you actually take an order. People's money will actually be spent, you will collect the funds, and you will then create the course very quickly and deliver it.

What's most important with the presale test is that you let everybody know, in very clear wording, that this is a presale launch.

You're testing your idea, but you're also launching at the same time. The presale test is a longer strategy. You have to let the customers who have purchased know roughly how long they will have to wait to start gaining access to whatever it is they are purchasing. It's a very ballsy approach, but if you feel confident about whatever it is you're creating, this is probably the best way to be able to test your idea.

You're actually making money while testing the idea, thus it's called the "Ballsy" Presale Test.

After you have tested and proven your price point, the next step is to launch!

CASE STUDY

NAME: Janet Murray
BUSINESS NAME: Soulful PR
WEBSITE: JanetMurray.co.uk

Background
Janet Murray spent 16 years writing and editing for national newspapers and magazines. In recent years she's primarily worked for the *Guardian*, but she has written for the *Times, Telegraph,*

Independent, Sun, Mirror, Daily Mail, and many glossy magazines. Janet has also made dozens of appearances on radio and television.

Early on in her career, she spotted something. Janet realized that most people were terrible at pitching to journalists, which meant most of their press releases or pitches got deleted and went unread. Janet decided she could teach them how to do it better. She now spends most of her time helping small business owners promote themselves in the media via her paid membership community, The Soulful PR Studio, running live events (including a big annual event called Soulful PR Live) and doing one-on-one and small group consulting.

Janet also has a blog, podcast (which is consistently in the Top 50 UK business podcasts), her book, *Your Press Release Is Breaking My Heart,* and her extensive media diary.

Establishing Authority

For Janet, it was very much about being able to "talk the talk." She wasn't a PR executive who just "thought" they knew what made a great story for a journalist, Janet knew exactly what made a great story because she was a journalist herself. Janet was the person who read the press releases and pitches that came in and decided what to follow up on and what to ignore. Janet is also not your average PR expert because she never actually worked in PR! That makes her far more memorable.

Janet started creating great content from an authoritative background. From the outset, she published free "how to" content on her blog showing people how to write press releases and email pitches, find journalists' contact details, and everything else she could think of that would help them get media coverage. Later Janet launched a podcast, a book, and a media diary. She is also very active on social media. Janet says it's about showing not telling. Anyone can say they're an expert, but a true expert shows it in the content they create.

Three Things to Grow Business Effectively

1. Creating high-quality free content that solves her customers' problems is at the heart of everything Janet does. Her podcast, which goes out twice a week, has been a huge investment (both in terms of time and money) but has been particularly powerful in terms of sending prospective customers her way. Janet says that by the time people have read her blog, listened to her podcast, taken part in her weekly Twitter "chat," watched her Facebook Lives, or consumed any of her other content, joining her membership, attending her event, buying her diary (or whatever else she is promoting at the time) feels like the natural next step. There's no need for a big sales pitch. When she soft-launched her membership community The Soulful PR Studio in December 2016 (that tricky period between Christmas and New Year when everyone says they haven't got any money), Janet got 100+ members from a casual Facebook post and a couple of emails.

2. Over the past few years Janet built a free Facebook community of 9,500 members. This has allowed her to have conversations with prospective customers, to find out what they're struggling with and how she can help. For example, last year Janet noticed people kept saying they were struggling with content ideas for their blogs and social media and to pitch into the press. She created a media diary—a desk diary that lists key awareness days, dates, and events small business owners can use to generate content ideas.

   Janet used the "Ballsy Presale" method to launch her diary. She got her designer to create a picture of the cover, created a simple landing page, added a PayPal button, and got a couple of hundred pre-orders from a Facebook post which validated her idea and gave her the confidence to go ahead and make the product. Since then Janet has sold thousands of her diaries.

Having a community that people identify with and feel part of is really powerful. Janet's members refer to themselves and each other as "soulies" and "soulsters." If people love being part of your community, they'll do your marketing for you, which is great.

3. It's certainly true that the money is in the list, and that's something Janet has really focused on. Janet tries to create ways to collect email addresses with every piece of content she creates, but one of the most successful pieces of email list-building she's done is her 10-day PR challenge.

    This is a 10-day email course that guides people through the basics of getting press coverage for their business. Janet designed it so it's easy for people to get a couple of early "wins" and she encourages conversation (i.e., invites people to email her with news of how they're doing). By the end of the 10-day challenge, people generally feel they've built a relationship with Janet, so offering them the opportunity to buy her book, join her next live event, or even join her membership feels like a natural next step rather than a sales pitch.

Most Profitable Monetization

Janet's most profitable part of her business is the membership community. Having a core group of clients who know, like, and trust you means you're not constantly looking for new customers. When you launch a new book, event, or mastermind program, your members are the ones who will be first in the queue to buy, and they'll tell all their friends, too. That's not to say it's an easy option—you need to cherish and care for this group of people and treat them like "family," but it makes everything else in your business so much easier.

Here's what Janet had to say about being a YOUPRENEUR:

The biggest advantage of being part of the Youpreneur Community is just that: community. I've met so many amazing business owners I've been inspired by over the years and have lost count of the ways I've worked with them; e.g., masterminding, appearing on each other's podcasts, guest teaching in each other's membership communities. I've particularly enjoyed meeting up with other Youpreneurs at live events. Knowing I can go to any event, pretty much anywhere in the world, and connect with other Youpreneurs is a good feeling.

12

THE LAUNCH FORMAT

OKAY, so you've figured out what you're going to sell. You've chosen your monetization method. Let's go back to the online course as an example product. You've built it out as part of your ever-expanding Youpreneur ecosystem and have priced it just right. You feel confident about it because you've tested the idea using one of the strategies that I've just gone through, and now it's actually time to launch your product (step 3).

What do you do? How do you get this product, this course, out to the public?

Great question. I'm glad you asked.

There are four parts to the launch:

- The pre-launch
- The launch
- The mid-launch
- The post-launch

The Pre-launch

The pre-launch starts before you launch your online course, obviously. It is designed to generate real buzz or interest about the course coming out. You're going to start talking about it everywhere. In today's world, you're really spoiled for choice here in regards to building buzz. You've got social media, you've got your email list, your blog, your podcast, YouTube video, and you've got live video.

Live video is absolutely huge for building pre-launch buzz, because it engages people right away.

Building buzz around your upcoming launch is paramount to initial launch success.

Buzz equals chitter-chatter from your tribe, in your own little ecosystem. People will start talking about your online course. The pre-launch buzz enables you to have built-in validation of what you're doing and what you're about to launch. Because if you start to see people get very excited about your launch, then you know what you're doing is going to work. You want people to start spreading the news, and start spreading the idea that the launch is coming.

The first strategy for buzz building is actually pretty easy. Just email your current subscribers and let them know your course is around the corner, and that it is going to be something they really need.

You build up the anticipation, and then you allow subscribers to get on your "VIP Waitlist." They can do this by clicking on a link on your site. Let them know they will have first access to the course, before anybody else. That creates a level of anticipation from your current subscribers and gets them to take early action. They've now shown real interest in your course by getting on the waitlist. They've got a little bit of skin in the game already, even though there is no monetary involvement yet.

You want to start creating this pre-launch buzz around four weeks before the actual launch of your product.

You set the launch date in stone, and then you stick to that date. This is a very important point, so don't forget it—stick to it! Once you start talking about a launch date publicly, if you move the goal posts and change that launch date, it's going to hurt you. It will not only hurt you from a sales perspective, but also from a reputation perspective. You don't want to do that. Keep the positive momentum going strong leading up to the launch.

Building buzz around your upcoming launch is **paramount to initial launch success.**

If you do this correctly, you're going to be creating buzz, getting chitter-chatter out there in the universe, and receiving some validation from people talking about what it is that you're going to be launching—your course. At this point it's all about building your VIP waitlist, which is hugely important to being able to hit the ground running and start making sales right out of the gate. All of this is meant to get people excited and anxious to the point where they'll want to click the *buy now* button the moment you send it to them.

My Number One Strategy for Building Buzz

I'm about to give you my number one strategy for building a VIP waitlist, so have your highlighter ready. Remember I said that live video was huge when it came to building buzz? This is exactly how I use live video when I'm in pre-launch mode, and I'm going to give you some numbers to show just how popular and how powerful live video can be.

When I launched the Youpreneur Community back in September 2015, I popped onto Periscope and did live video broadcasts every day for a month before the actual launch. I talked about anything and everything to do with personal branding and building a business around your brand—because that's what Youpreneur is all about. That's what my community does. It serves personal brand entrepreneurs who want to become the go-to source in their industry.

Every day I would get on and spend about 15 to 20 minutes going through pieces of content on pretty much everything I've discussed thus far in this book.

Once the launch date was set in stone, I started building my VIP waitlist. I had a little notecard with the web address written on it that I wanted people to visit to hop on the waitlist. Because it was a live video, I would wave that notecard in front of my camera several times throughout each of those live presentations. You want to pick a URL that's short and sweet, and one that people can remember without having to write it down.

During the course of that month, we had over 600 people join that VIP launch list. Not only did I have my normal email subscriber list, but now I had 600-plus people who had skin in the game and had essentially said, "Yes, I validate your idea, Chris. I like the sound of what you're putting together. I want to know about this offer before anybody else!"

My Launch Numbers on Day One

So, what did that mean for my launch? Well, here are some numbers for you. On launch day of September 1, 2015, I did a 45-minute live launch Periscope broadcast to my VIP launch list. In that time, we brought in 86 sales directly from that one broadcast. We added 36 annual members, and 50 monthly members. We generated live revenue of just over $18,000 in that 45-minute broadcast. I did the broadcast live, launched my product, made some money, and then went to bed.

Here's the interesting part. I did the live video launch in the evening from the Philippines. That meant, because of the 12-hour difference in time zones, it was early morning on the East Coast of the US. The next morning, I woke up, and my wife said to me, "You know what? You should do another broadcast. You should do another launch right now for everybody on the West Coast of America." My wife was right, of course. She reminded me that 54 percent of my audience is in the US, and a big portion of my US market was probably asleep when I did my initial launch.

So, I went live for a second time, essentially did the exact same broadcast I did the night before, and it brought in another 29 sales, which amounted to another $4,000. In less than

24 hours, I brought in $22,405 off that VIP live launch list. That's hitting the ground running right there.

Who doesn't want that? Putting effort in before you launch can set you up for incredible results from day one.

THE LAUNCH CYCLE

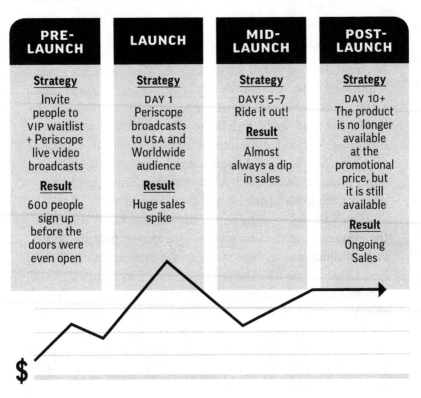

PRE-LAUNCH	LAUNCH	MID-LAUNCH	POST-LAUNCH
Strategy	**Strategy**	**Strategy**	**Strategy**
Invite people to VIP waitlist + Periscope live video broadcasts	DAY 1 Periscope broadcasts to USA and Worldwide audience	DAYS 5–7 Ride it out!	DAY 10+ The product is no longer available at the promotional price, but it is still available
Result	**Result**	**Result**	
600 people sign up before the doors were even open	Huge sales spike	Almost always a dip in sales	
			Result
			Ongoing Sales

The Launch

How long is your launch going to be? You want to set a definitive time frame for it—10 days to two weeks is normal. However, I think you'll find that two weeks for a launch becomes quite tiring, and therefore, you'll probably only ever do a two-week launch once in your life. Believe me, I did it once and didn't like it.

All of my launches are now 10 days. I'll have that pre-launch period of a month, when the buzz is being built, so I can hit the ground running to make lots of sales out of the gate. Then, within a 10-day period, I market to the world that my latest offering is live.

I set emails to go out at strategic times throughout the launch—usually four to five emails in total in the 10-day period. I'll definitely pop on to live video a couple of times as well—usually right at the beginning of the launch and again on the last day. I might even do a webinar too. More on this later!

This launch seems like it will work like clockwork, right? The truth is, it will—as long as you plan it properly. Almost every launch I've ever done in a similar format has panned out. Sure, some launches have brought in more money than others, but the flow of the launches themselves has been very similar from one offering to the next.

The Mid-launch

At around day five to day seven, right in the middle of your launch, you'll have a lull in sales. It's common for this to happen. Everybody experiences it.

What you want to do is develop a mid-launch bonus of some kind. This can be an additional training video, an e-book PDF download, or maybe even some type of equipment you can include. For instance, if you're teaching a course on creating live video, you could say, "For anybody who buys today, we're going to send you this microphone that you can use in your live videos." Whatever it is, you need to offer something extra of value for about 48 hours in the middle of your launch that will ultimately minimize that predictable lull in sales.

I always favor digital content as a bonus, because I want something that's super easy to deliver. But it really depends on what you're all about. I've actually seen people utilize live events very well as part of the mid-launch bonus. They may say, "If you buy in the next 48 hours, you'll have access to a live mastermind event that I will be holding in the first quarter of next year."

Obviously, you've got to make sure that anybody who has purchased prior to the offer is going to get the mid-launch bonus too. Otherwise, you'll have lots of upset customers on your hands.

As the 10 days start to wind down and you get to the point of ending the launch, you'll find about 50 percent of your sales will come in the last 24 hours. At this point, you want to go really hard, talking about it everywhere online.

Invest more time and effort in the last 24 hours of a launch than you do in the first 24 hours!

You may want to launch a podcast episode that last day or go live on Facebook or YouTube or whatever your choice of live video platform is. You want to really hammer home the fact that your launch is closing and time is running out for people to buy. This builds urgency. You could say something like, *Hey, this is it! You've got less than 24 hours to get this course before we close the doors!* (Or before the price goes up, depending on your strategy.)

Whatever you're going to use to create urgency—shutting the sales down at a specific time or raising the price—you

Invest more time and effort in the last **24 hours of a launch** than you do in the first 24 hours!

want to definitely email your whole list again to keep momentum going. Start a conversation with your list about it. Share some of the early testimonials you got from the people who have already purchased. Send screenshots of people talking about your product or service on social media or inside your private forums. Then, with literally three to four hours left in the launch, send them another email.

Yes, you're going to email people at night, and you're going to say to them, *Hey, we're about to close the doors on this. This is the last time you're going to hear about this from me; it's been a pleasure spending time and hearing all the great stories, but this is your last chance to get involved. We're closing the doors soon!*

Here's where I'm going to get up on my soapbox a little. It's up to you whether you want to say you're closing the doors, raising the price, or taking away certain bonuses. Whatever you choose, do what you said you would do—when you said it would be done.

You will get people emailing you with one excuse or another as to why they couldn't buy before the time on the offer elapsed. They'll ask you to push them through, to make an exception. Don't do it. The fact is, they've had more than enough time—your launch has been 10 days. This is a chance for you to stand your ground (which every entrepreneur needs to do from time to time) and to use this as a mindset training opportunity. They'll buy before the deadline next time. I promise.

The Post-launch

Now, I have "closed the doors" to end launches in the past. I don't do it anymore. Honestly, the more I think about it, the more I shake my head with astonishment that I ever bought into the tactic in the first place.

The fact is that closing the doors on offerings has been "the norm" for quite some time, and many people believe that it's still the best tactic for online entrepreneurs selling digital products and access to memberships.

But I don't buy into this anymore.

Think about it. If you were hungry and went to a restaurant for something to eat, and when you got there, it was closed with a sign that said it wouldn't be open again until next month, what would you do? Would you wait a month to eat? Or would you find another restaurant and eat right there and then, spending your money elsewhere?

I'll tell you what I did in exactly that situation. I was all dressed up for an evening out with my wife in Hong Kong, and we were very much looking forward to trying out a high-end restaurant that had come highly recommended. When we got there, however, the place was closed—just a sign on the door telling us to come back another time. Well, we couldn't do that— we were in Hong Kong for just a short time to begin with, and we were hungry *then*, not another time. So we found another restaurant and ate there instead.

Don't make this mistake. Don't make people wait three, four, or six months just because of your launch schedule. There always has to be a

> Grab another of our Youpreneur Process Blueprints! This one will show you How to Launch Your Product Successfully. Just visit **Youpreneur.com/ReadersOnly**

way for them to be able to get what you've got, because if they don't get it when they need it, and from YOU, they're going to go and spend money with someone else.

Instead, run promotions. You get the value-add of a time-sensitive launch and can use bonuses or offer a discount. Just be sure that whatever you're offering in your promotion, your existing customers either get the same bonuses or are paying less than your discounted offer.

Sample Launch Timeline

To wrap up this section, I'm going to share with you the exact timeline that I used recently on a promotional launch we did for Virtual Staff Finder. You can plug and play as much of this as you want in your next launch and hopefully see some great results.

As you can see, it's not necessarily rocket science. It's about personally getting in front of my community at the start of the launch, then again in the middle, and right at the end. At all other times, I'm staying front of mind via social media mentions, emails, and any other activities I decide to throw into the mix, like a webinar, for example.

SAMPLE LAUNCH TIMELINE

DAY 1

- 9 a.m. Email List with Promotion Offer
- 10 a.m. Live Video on Facebook Page
- Social Media Mentions (All Platforms)

DAY 2

- Twitter and Facebook Mentions
- Graphics on Instagram, Instagram Stories

DAY 3

- Email "Unopened" Subscribers
- Live Video on Periscope
- Live Video on Instagram

DAY 4

- Twitter and Facebook Mentions
- Graphics on Instagram, Instagram Stories

DAY 5

- Email Mid-launch 24-Hour Bonus (Swipe Files)
- Promote Mid-launch Bonus on Social

DAY 6

- Twitter and Facebook Mentions
- Graphics on Instagram, Instagram Stories

DAY 7

- 10 a.m. Live Webinar Presentation
- 12 noon Post-webinar Reply to Facebook Page

DAY 8

- Twitter and Facebook Mentions
- Graphics on Instagram, Instagram Stories

DAY 9

- 9 a.m. Email List (Offer Ending Tomorrow)
- 10 a.m. Live Video on Facebook Page
- Retarget Page Visitors on Facebook Ads

DAY 10

- 9 a.m. Email List (Minus Tagged Buyers)
- 10 a.m. Live Video on All Platforms
- 6 p.m. Email List (Last Chance!)
- Twitter and Facebook Mentions
- Graphics on Instagram, Instagram Stories
- Retarget Page Visitors on Facebook Ads

13

ONGOING MARKETING

AVE you ever noticed how some businesses seem to fade away almost as fast as they showed up, and how others seem to stay around forever? I believe the difference comes down to something very simple. Some business owners are focused on the quick win—get in, launch a product, make some money, and move onto the next thing. People and businesses like this don't stick around for very long.

Business owners who focus on long-term monetization strategies seem to be around year after year.

Becoming a true Youpreneur isn't a business that you're just going to open and close tomorrow. It's one that you want to sink into and focus on for the long game.

In the last chapter, I talked about options for ending a product launch. You could choose to close the doors completely and take away the opportunity for people to buy whatever it is you've just launched. Or you might just increase the cost of the product or service, or take away the bonuses you offered, which means the product is still going to be available for people to buy.

When you keep the product active, it gives you the opportunity to consistently get in front of your audience and create an ongoing marketing plan. As with any long-game plan, you've got to remain flexible, because some of the things you do might end up working out better than others.

There are four main areas I focus in on when it comes to my ongoing marketing, above and beyond the creation of high-value, original content on a weekly basis. Make no mistake, the ongoing creation and marketing of your content should remain at the very heart of what you do as a Youpreneur.

However, in addition to all that juicy content, I also use live video, webinars, paid advertising, and email marketing with a long-game attitude. So let's zoom in a little bit on these four key areas.

Live Video Coaching

Live video coaching is when you get online on a consistent basis (perhaps weekly to begin with) and provide coaching or training—for free. You could do this with Facebook Live, Instagram Live, or Periscope. Use whatever you are most comfortable with so that you are consistently delivering content to your audience in this format.

The video content should not be difficult to create. What I do is focus in on one major tactic or strategy per individual broadcast. And then I follow a simple three-step process for when I go live:

1. I use one question as the title of the broadcast.
2. I answer that one question and only that question.
3. I do this by creating three bullet talking points.

All you need to do is figure out what one question you want to answer, then you focus in on answering that question with three talking points. The three bullet points are just there to prompt you.

Don't overthink this one. Make it easy for yourself. Before I go live I get a Post-it note, and I'll jot down the question, what the overall answer is going to be, and then the three bullet points that make up that answer. Then I'll either stick that Post-it note to the side of my phone if I'm broadcasting via my iPhone, or on the monitor underneath the camera if I'm broadcasting via my desktop. I make sure to position my notes so they are out of the view of the camera so it doesn't look like I'm reading them.

These are quick, to-the-point videos. They should only go on for an absolute maximum of 10 to 15 minutes. If you've got a good enough size live audience, then you could throw in five minutes of Q&A after the training. The whole point of doing live video is twofold.

Number one, you want to engage with your live audience. In other words, you want to interact with your prospects. These are people who could potentially either opt in to your email list or end up buying something that you might offer that's relevant to what it is you're talking about live.

The other reason why you want to do these videos on a regular basis is that consistency builds what I call *live loyalty*. This is an audience that enjoys watching you live. If they know that you're going to be on at 9 p.m. every day, Monday through Friday, they're going to do their best to tune in live every single time. The reason why is people are creatures of habit. This is why television shows become so successful. You never have to wonder when your favorite show will be on. You always know it will be on the same time and on the same channel.

Publishing consistent live video training is almost like having your own TV training show: people will become loyal to you. They tune in at the same time every week or every day, whatever you decide your schedule will be. That consistency builds loyalty, but it also helps people feel comfortable being on the receiving end of that transmission. You become their go-to person for the content they're looking for.

If you say you're going to be going live every Monday, Wednesday, and Friday, just make sure that you are there on time.

Consistency is everything when it comes to content creation and marketing.

Another important aspect of live video coaching is you have to engage with your live viewers properly. You want to always remember to ask for those hearts, ask for the likes, ask for comments and questions, and ask for them to share your call to action. Engaging your audience gets them involved. When your audience is involved, they will talk about what they are doing. You see this happen with most reality shows. People start to follow who they like, and they vote for their favorites. That engagement prompts them to talk about the show with their friends. Now the friends want to watch too.

You can create that same viral feel if you engage your audience properly.

Webinar Presentations

Webinars are nothing new. They haven't just come on to the scene in the last year or so. They've been around for a long, long time. Some people say that because of the dawn of live video, webinars are losing their footing in the marketing space. I don't agree with that. I think webinars still work very well for a couple of reasons.

Unlike live video, where nobody needs to actually register to see one of your live video broadcasts on social media, people must register to get the link for a webinar to be able to view the presentation. So that enables you to create or *grow your email list,* because people have to register with their email addresses to actually get access.

Another reason a webinar still works is that your prospects, by opting into one, have put some skin in the game. While it's not monetary, they did "give up" their email address. With this little bit of skin, your audience is more likely to actually pay attention to what you say in that webinar.

When people are on your webinar and you are providing content for free to them, that's a captive audience. And yes, 95 percent of free webinars end with some kind of a pitch for

Consistency is everything when it comes to content creation and marketing.

a product or a service. Now, that doesn't mean everybody is going to buy, because quite frankly, the conversion rates are still quite small for webinars. The fact is that because you're providing great training content for them, with a bit of luck, that'll help move the needle for them in some way, shape, or form. So even if they don't buy today, they've opted in, they've turned up, they've gotten to know you and your style and what you can help them with, so they might end up actually buying from you at some point in the future.

Hence, the long-game focus.

Paid Webinars for Additional Monetization

The other side of the webinar world, and this is developing very quickly, is paid webinars. I think paid webinars are actually going to be the real future of webinars. They work way better for us content creators because you are charging people upfront. It's like you're selling a digital product, but the product isn't actually created yet.

Your audience can't get their hands on it right now, but they will at the specific time on the specific date that you say the webinar will be taking place.

The only difference between the free webinar and the paid one is—you guessed it— people are paying to see this one. You could charge a nominal fee like $20 to $25, or if the webinar is going to be a two- or three-hour presentation, you could charge a lot more than that. The fact is, now your audience has got even more skin in the game. You will see the turn-up rate between free webinars and paid webinars are complete and utter polar opposites.

And there is the added benefit of paid webinars taking the stress off the presenter. This is one of the reasons why I believe paid webinars are the future. They eliminate the pressure of having to pitch something at the end to make the presentation worthwhile. If you are charging people upfront to get access to the webinar, obviously you don't need to have an offer at the end as well. That doesn't mean you can't do an upsell of some kind, but almost all of the paid webinars I've been part of had no pitch at the end.

It's Not a Tech Headache Anymore

A lot of people stay away from doing webinars because of the setup required. Quite frankly, tech is the biggest stumbling block for most people, myself included. I didn't do webinars for the longest time, even though I really wanted to, because of the tech setup. But the fact is nowadays we've got services that make it almost a tech-zero situation and very seamless to actually put on a webinar event.

The first one I recommend is GoToWebinar, the second one is Zoom, and the third would be Webinar Ninja. I've used all of them, but I prefer GoToWebinar. However, it is the most expensive option. All three will get you up and running, so do your due diligence here, and find the solution that's right for you.

So, the tech side of things is probably not your most important concern when doing a webinar. Focus on your presentation and your closing, if you are doing an offer at the end of your free webinar. These are the most important elements.

Your presentation needs to be strong. Make sure you spend some time on your slide deck. Make visuals, keep them on brand point, and make them nice and attractive. You'll need a lot of visuals to keep people's attention. Flipping from one slide to another creates movement in the presentation and gives the viewer something new to look at. I would say in a 45-minute webinar presentation, you probably need about 100 or so slides.

Want a perfect, step-by-step guide to putting on your first webinar? Oh, okay—don't say I never gave you anything! Grab another one of my Process Blueprints here: **Youpreneur.com/ReadersOnly**

It sounds like a lot, but with today's attention span, it's a must. Otherwise, they'll be off checking email, looking at their phone, and everything else other than watching your webinar.

What you leave your audience with is always critical. If you are doing a free webinar, or if you are offering some kind of upsell on your paid webinar, it's very important to practice the "closing" over and over again before you actually get on live with your attendees.

If you want to sell anything to anybody, preparation is king all the way. Every day.

Quite frankly, **tech is the biggest stumbling block** for most people, myself included.

Paid Advertising

Chances are you've probably heard the phrase "you've got to pay to play." It couldn't be any truer than when it comes to advertising on the Internet. The world of real, organic advertising has definitely disappeared. And, because of the way that Facebook is building out its advertising platform as their number one revenue stream, paid advertising seems to be setting up to be here for a long time.

People often think that advertising online is going to be very expensive, but it doesn't have to be. Depending on how you decide to market—and what you decide to advertise and why—paid advertising does not need to be expensive, and certainly is not nearly as costly as it once was. It doesn't matter if you're just advertising to get people to your content on your blog or podcast, or if you're sending them to a landing page to get opt-ins for your mailing list, or possibly even pointing them to the sales page of your latest product launch.

Online advertising can be effective and reasonably priced. It's not something you should shy away from.

Facebook Advertising

As for me, I recommend three major ways to get involved in paid advertising online. The first one is with Facebook ads. For me, this is the way forward. Their ad platform is just so incredibly intuitive, and you can really dial down the demographic you're looking to advertise to. If you want to hit males 25 to 35 years old living on the East Coast of the United States that are into health and fitness... you can set your ad reach to do just that. You can actually search out and advertise to people based on the specific job positions they hold, or the industries they work in, or even their interests or pastimes.

So if you are a professional skateboard company selling skateboard accessories, such as decks, wheels, trucks, and everything else that skateboarders need, you can target your ad right down to anybody within any area of the world within any specific niche and pitch your skateboard products to them directly through Facebook. It's a very powerful and incredibly targeted way to advertise. Especially for local retail businesses.

But, for us Youpreneurs, it's all about keeping ourselves in front of our followers online. As I mentioned earlier on, you can upload your email list to Facebook, and then, for next to nothing, retarget those subscribers directly on the social media platform and send them to content you produce as well as your sales pages and more.

Google AdWords

If you do a Google search, right at the top of that search's results page you'll usually see between three to six listings that people have actually paid to have appear.

These are ads from Google AdWords. They are a bit more expensive than Facebook ads but still work very well because people are using Google on a daily basis for the majority of their online searches. So if you want links to your content to appear at the top of Google searches, then you may want to consider using AdWords for some of your advertising.

It stands to reason that the more competitive the niche you're in, the more expensive it'll be to utilize this type of paid advertising—but in smaller, less competitive markets, especially if you're targeting longer keywords (think "smoothie bar in Wimbledon, London," instead of "smoothie bar in London"), it can be very beneficial.

Retargeting Adverts

The third method for online advertising I recommend is called retargeting. A company you might want to check out is AdRoll. What AdRoll does is track what people search for online and then target certain types of ads to that person. So, depending on what page people have visited on your website, you can then actually retarget those visitors by producing little banner graphic ads, which will pop up all over the Internet on any website that is participating in AdRoll's partner program.

Imagine visiting a webpage for Mother's Day gifts, but you don't buy anything. Then for the next few weeks, every now and then you'll see these adverts pop up as you visit other websites. Everywhere you look there's another ad for that Mother's Day website that you visited. That's the power of retargeting. You capture people's interests and then place ads right in front of them, over and over again. It's a little scary, and a bit stalkerish, but it works very well. Like Google AdWords, it's not as cheap as Facebook ads, but definitely worth doing. Adverts are particularly effective for promoting limited time-frame offers, like book launches, product launches, or live events.

No matter what direction you choose to go in with paid advertising, be sure you focus on the images when setting up your ads, especially if you go down the retargeting route. Images are everything.

You've got to have high-quality photography to grab people's attention. Stay away from using stock images that everybody else is using if you can. Use your own proprietary photos whenever possible. This will make your ads unique to your business. Paying attention to the types of images you use is important because it can mean the difference between an extra two or three percent on click-through conversions. If you're using better-quality images, you may see an increase in your clicks, and more clicks mean bigger potential for making more money.

It's extremely, extremely important that you stick with your brand when creating paid advertising. I've worked with some ad management firms that were completely off-target with not only the images, but also with the colors, the fonts, and the style of the ads they produced for my business. Guess what? Those ads didn't work for me.

Always be testing, but at the end of the day, without a doubt, don't deviate from your brand colors, always use your logo, always use the same fonts and even the same language. People take miniature snapshots in the back of their mind whenever they see messaging from you.

What I mean by that is you'll find that some of your taglines and marketing statements will work better than others. You get to find out what works best by just testing and seeing what the data tells you. At the end of the day, branding is everything. I have talked about consistency in putting together your content, delivering it, and keeping your message on point, but your branding has to be ultra consistent when you're spending money to get in front of people.

Even if they don't buy, even if they don't click on that link or that message, they're still taking those little miniature photographs in their mind. They're capturing what you have to offer, what you're all about, and how you project your business and your brand—all of that could mean that they'll be more likely to click next time.

Ongoing Email Marketing

The fourth area of ongoing marketing is email marketing. What you want to do with your email marketing is put it on autopilot as much as you possibly can. Work on building out your autoresponder to the point where you've got months and months of content prewritten, preloaded, and timed so your emails are sent on a consistent schedule automatically. This helps ensure that people who actually do invest time in reading your emails stay on your email list for longer, and it guarantees they're consistently getting high-quality, valuable content from you.

My auto-responder allows me to program out emails for approximately six months. That's at least six months' worth of content that you'll get from me, and once I have the system set up, I don't ever have to actually do anything to make that happen. Sometimes you'll get an email from me once a week throughout those six months. Sometimes it might be every other week. From time to time, you could get emails a couple of times a week, depending on what the content is that I'm serving up to you.

You have to understand this—the money truly is in your email list.

Think about it—the more qualified, engaged people you have on your list, the bigger and more turned on your audience is going to be. However, there will come a time when the size of your list starts to potentially overwhelm you—this is a good problem to have, obviously. But, nonetheless, still a problem. This is where segmentation comes into play.

Segmenting Your List

Whenever possible, you want to segment your list. This will help you get specific in the messaging sent to each group of people. You can segment your list based on where people are in their journey within your industry. Maybe they're beginners, intermediate, or more advanced. You may want to send a beginner a different message than you would send to someone who is more advanced. I touched on this a bit earlier on when we talked about growing email lists.

Segmenting your email list helps you target your potential customers in a much more conducive and profitable manner.

To segment your list properly, you can simply provide links for your subscribers to click on to show what their interest levels are, or if you're going to be surveying them, you can segment your list individually based on their answers. However you want to do it, the important thing is that you do it, not only on an as-needed basis, but on a long-term basis as well.

I've hammered this idea of playing the long game quite a bit in this book, and I'm going to pound on it a bit more for really the last time here. Email marketing is crucial in succeeding at the long game.

Nothing you do will be as important to the long-term success of your online business as building a highly engaged and targeted email list. If you engage with your audience on a regular basis, if you spend time converting clients who are now part of your Youpreneur ecosystem on a regular basis, if you answer questions consistently, if you often hang out on social media with your people, all of that—everything you do—should tie back to your email list.

You've got to get people on your list, and you've got to get them to stay on your list.

You do that by adopting that play-the-long-game mindset of consistently showing up, caring, and always serving up really high-quality, valuable content that's going to continue to help people for many, many months and years to come.

Segmenting your email list helps you target your potential customers in a much more **conducive and profitable manner**.

CASE STUDY

NAME: Amy Schmittauer
BUSINESS NAME: Vlog Boss Studios
WEBSITE: SavvySexySocial.com

Background

Amy likes to create things that surprise and delight people. When she discovered video blogging in 2007, she felt like she finally found the perfect creative outlet for this. Even though Amy was attending school for political science and working in an aligned position successfully, the industry of vlogging and online communications pulled her attention so greatly that she decided to leave Plan A completely and work for herself.

Amy said, "I didn't have anything in my arsenal except ambition, passion, hard work, and a history of being a computer nerd as a kid. I'm self-taught and peer-inspired in every aspect of my field and love the fact that every day I have to learn something new to continue to be good enough to live the life I want."

Establishing Authority

Amy says that knowing her strongest communication strength and using it often is a key contributor to establishing her credibility. She stays away from everyone's favorite excuse: "My market is oversaturated." Using that excuse is a great way to convince yourself not to show up. Instead of deciding all the trailblazers before her were enough for the industry, she decided she should have a voice right next to them. In order to do that, she leaned into what her upper hand is in communication, and that's vlogging. She showed up three days a week religiously for three years straight to teach and share her opinion in her vlog. Video was what she was best at in terms of communication style, while the level of consistency was the thing lots of people never get right. By conquering them both, she nailed her name to the industry.

A second contributing factor for Amy's established authority status is meeting people, online and offline. Creating content isn't enough, but it's a massive piece of explaining what you stand for. But if no one sees it... who cares?

She took the time to get to know the people in and around her industry who could lift her higher and help her achieve exposure. Whether they were a potential customer or a lifetime subscriber, they mattered.

Three Things to Grow Business Effectively

1. Consistently leveraging YouTube video content marketing. Amy's goal in creating her content is to help other people go after the life they want and provide actionable tips to help them make that happen. She continues to publish regularly on YouTube with this advice while also offering a behind the scenes look at how she's going after the life she wants.

2. Writing a book. It may seem weird that someone who creates a video series would be asked so passionately by her audience to write a book, but that's what happened to Amy. The community spoke about what they wanted, and she listened. What she didn't anticipate was how much credibility becoming an author offers someone because it's an action held in such high regard for thought leadership.

3. Tracking contacts diligently for follow up. You can't assume people will remember you every time their need arises for what you do. You have to keep showing up in their life. Amy sends check-in emails to at least 20 people a week when her

schedule allows for it. If her schedule is too busy, she at least looks through her social networks and sends direct message notes congratulating or giving props on something she sees they are up to. With this personal touch and her content always popping up in social feeds, she becomes memorable. Every single touch point counts.

Most Profitable Monetization

Amy's most profitable activity in her business is coaching. People just want your time and expertise. If you offer it and you're good at what you do, you can charge a premium for it.

Here's what Amy had to say about what excites her the most about being a personal brand business owner:

I feel like I'm actually in charge of my life. If something happens to my industry or the market that changes demand, I can adapt quickly and continue to prove my relevance. It's hard work, but I wouldn't change a second of it.

14

THE POWER OF A HAPPY CUSTOMER

CAN make an argument that the most important aspect of any business is not marketing or sales. And it's not product development or branding—it's customer service. The funny thing is that whenever the topic of customer service comes up, most business owners' eyes glaze over, and they mentally move on to the next topic. To be a successful Youpreneur, you need to change your position on customer service and take a proactive role in keeping your customers as happy as possible.

Before you start pitching your customers, you want to know what they really want. The sales process is usually one of the more intimidating and trickier aspects for entrepreneurs when it comes to business, which is why it's important to get into that customer mindset and learn how to create the right customer experience to create brand loyalty.

Once you know what they want, and have created that loyalty, it's time for you to flex that sales muscle.

Making Customer Service a Priority

A few years ago, I had a conversation with a coaching client of mine. When I asked him what his three main focuses in his business were, he said, "Well number one, I'm always focusing on getting new customers. Number two is about making sure that my existing customers are happy all the time. And number three, I focus in on making sure my team is happy, because they're helping me run my business."

The team is where customer service begins and ends. It's got nothing to do with your customers, per se, it's about how you train your team, and how you treat your team. It's about whether your team members are either excited, happy, and loyal, or whether they're floating in a completely different direction.

So I turned this client upside down. I said, "Well, you've got it all wrong, my friend. Number one, most important, is your team. And that's purely because of the customer service element of your business. If your team is happy, then they're going to do a better job when it comes to customer service." I said, "Number two, you should be focusing on your existing customers. Number three is focusing on getting new customers."

Why should you focus on your existing customers before going after new ones?

It's way easier to continue to get a "yes" from existing customers than it is to get the "first yes" from a prospective one.

I talked a little bit about this earlier on in regards to membership sites as a business model for your ecosystem, because you're getting a recurring "yes" on a monthly or quarterly basis.

It's way easier to **continue to get a "yes" from existing customers** than it is to get the "first yes" from a prospective one.

When it comes to growing your Youpreneur-based business, you want to make sure you focus on (in this order):

1. Your Team
2. Existing Customers
3. New Customers

A lot of companies out there are taking their customers for granted. That's a major mistake on their part. Happy customers are a cornerstone of a successful business. This is why I think making customer service a major focus for your business should be a priority.

It doesn't matter whether you're a coach, speaker, or consultant who is working closely with private clients, event organizers, and high-level customers—or if you're a huge multinational organization that is dealing with customers all over the world.

Don't *ever* take your customers for granted.

Make Making Contact Easy

Customers want to be able to reach you, so one key to making them happy is providing a number of different ways they can contact you. It's not just your support email address that you have to worry about anymore. If you have a Twitter account, you better make sure that it's manned. If you have a Facebook page, be sure your customer service team is looking after that also. Have your team really make customer experience a priority so you know that when customers need you, they can reach out to you at any time.

Protect the perception of your customer service.

People will almost always form an overall opinion of your service based on one interaction.

Do all you can to make sure that each customer experience is a good one. For instance, if you're not going to have anybody working over the Christmas holiday, tell your customers in advance, via an email or a message on your website, that if they contact you during that period of time, they're not going to hear back until after the holiday. Being proactive in protecting your reputation is a great way to make sure you always have a good one to protect.

You want to hear from your customers. Don't listen to people when they tell you otherwise. A lot of experts say that when you don't hear from your customers that's a good thing, but I would rather have good, engaged, and happy customers than ones that are not active at all. I want to talk to my customers so I can hear about their issues or even to get some praise from them too. If you don't know what's working and what's *not* working, you're going to be stuck playing the guessing game.

I like to make calls every now and then to my existing customers. These are calls that I, myself, make to people chosen randomly just to engage them in communication. By the way, the word *call* doesn't necessarily mean a phone call.

I could use Skype or something as simple as a Facebook message or direct tweet. The point is I like to reach out to my customers on a regular basis. You can schedule this contact to make it easy to maintain, and you don't have to reach out to all of your customers at one time. Set up a specific time, once a week or once a month, select a number of people, and simply contact them. Do it just to make sure they're happy regardless of where they are in your process. If they've got questions for you, then go ahead and answer them, right there and then. That's how you take a proactive approach to making sure your customers stay around year after year.

As much as I want you to be engaged with your customers, you can eliminate so much customer service volume in terms of ticket requests, support emails, social media questions, and so on by having a really well thought out and put together FAQ (frequently asked questions) section on your website. You can

People will **almost always** form an overall opinion of your service based on **one interaction**.

include a whole bunch of info in there, such as warranty information, exchange policies, guarantees, all that type of stuff.

Showing Up for Complaints

With that said, it's not enough just to give your customers a way to contact you or to engage them in some way. More importantly, you have to show up and actively face whatever they bring to your attention. I've talked about it a little bit before, and actually my very good friend, Jay Baer, from Convince and Convert, covers this beautifully in his book *Hug Your Haters*, where he discusses handling social media complaints, amongst other things.

Being proactive when handling complaints is paramount to a Youpreneur's reputation.

Several times, I've been in the position where I have complained. I'm British, after all. We like to do two things better than any other nation in the world. Number one—happily stand in queues, and number two—complain. I often say if complaining were an Olympic event, we would win gold every four years. In fact, I don't think any other nation would even compete! They'd just hand over the gold to the UK.

But seriously, handling your social media complaints is crucial, because social can go real bad real quick—as we learned earlier on, thanks to Amy and her Baking Company.

I once flew with Philippine Airlines twice in a 10-day period between Cebu and Manila. Manila is the capital and main business district of the country. Cebu is the fastest-growing economic zone in the country and a place that I called home from 2004, until I moved back to the UK recently.

Imagine this: two times within the space of 10 days, I'm a business class passenger sitting in the lounge, and the Wi-Fi is down. It's not acceptable for Wi-Fi to be down in a business class lounge twice within a 10-day period. Not only that, but on my second trip, there was a leaky roof in the lounge. Drip, drip, drip, drip, and no one was taking care of it.

I did what any modern-day passenger would do: I went to social media to complain about it. The first time, I complained on Twitter and I got an obviously standard reply saying, *Thank you for your complaint; we will take care of it.* Obviously they did not, because a week and a half later I was there, and the Wi-Fi was still down.

The second time I went to their Facebook page, and I wrote out a couple of paragraphs and posted my complaint there. What did they do?

Did they reply to me in a timely fashion? No.

Did they reply to me at all? No.

Did I get completely ignored? Yes.

But what made it even worse is they deleted my complaint entirely from their page. That did not leave me with a warm and fuzzy feeling in regards to flying with Philippine Airlines. Since that day I have never, ever flown with them again.

Not only did they not handle my social media complaint, but they completely ignored it, and therefore lost a customer for life—a customer, quite frankly, who used to travel between Cebu and Manila on a monthly basis for business. Now I give my money to their competitors.

Be sure you are really showing up and addressing your customers' complaints. You don't want them giving the money they would usually invest with you to someone else.

Turning Complainers into Champions

There is no doubt that customers like to complain, but the reverse side of that coin is that when you work to turn those complainers around, sometimes they go from being a dissatisfied customer to being your biggest champion.

I have talked about the concept of wanting to build raving fans who share about you to their friends and all around the Internet. Those customers can say good things about you or they can trash talk you. What a lot of people don't understand is that when you overdeliver on your customer service and you're honest and you keep things simple, you actually become seen as even more of an expert.

The interaction you have in your customer service environment will almost always shape into an additional experience for your customers.

I think a lot of people miss that point. Customer service is way more than just replying to people. It's almost become, as Jay Baer would say, a spectator sport. You, as the company, selling customers whatever it is that you're selling to them, have to

The interaction you have in your **customer service environment** will almost always shape into an additional experience for your customers.

become a spectator. You've got to become proactive in keeping an eye on how your customers are talking about you.

Remember, earlier we talked about your brand being what people say about you when you're not around. Well, this is it on steroids, right here.

More than 80 percent of the companies out there servicing people around the world on a daily basis through their products and services think they deliver great customer service. But the fact is that probably less than 10 percent of them actually do. That's the reality. So just by doing the work upfront and having that framework in place for you to be able to handle complaints, privately or publicly, will put you way ahead of the competition.

My Three-Sentence Email Rule

I've been blessed to build a thriving business based around an equally thriving community online. A community that knows me well, and therefore knows that I'm all about P2P and interacting with them.

Because of this, I get a lot of email. To handle the sheer volume, a few years ago I adopted a three-sentence email rule. This is actually not just for customer service, but also for all email correspondence in general. If you ever send me an email, and you can do so whenever you like at Chris@ChrisDucker.com, at the end of my email response as part of my signature you will see something along the lines of, *Why is this email three sentences or less? Click here to find out!*

When my email recipient clicks on that link, they go to my website where I talk about productivity for the modern-day entrepreneur and why every email that I reply to has got three sentences or fewer. Time is money and I want to honor my time as well as yours. I want not only to reply to all my emails, but to do so in a timely fashion. The same three-sentence rule can be used for day-to-day productivity, answering general customer service questions, support tickets, handling complaints, and email requests of any kind. When you have that three-sentence rule in place, you're a lot more consistent and concise in the way you respond to any correspondence that comes through.

And you're saving time.

Remember, when you say "yes" to something, you're instantly saying "no" to something else.

So being efficient with email is a good thing. You're also giving people something to talk about. I've lost count of how many times I've heard somebody mention my three-sentence email rule on podcasts, in blog posts, or just via social media sharing.

The bottom line is really understanding that time is money not only for you, but also for your customers, and that putting customer service above and beyond marketing and coming out with cool content will actually serve you much, much better. It will put you a hop and a skip ahead of your competitors, because chances are they're not making customer service a focus for their business.

If you do so, you shall be rewarded for it.

CASE STUDY

NAME: Lisa Woodruff
BUSINESS NAME: Organize 365
WEBSITE: Organize365.com

Background
On the eve of her 40th birthday, Lisa K. Woodruff was determined to start one more business.

The previous year Lisa had filed nine different income streams for tax purposes. She found out that she was good at creating jobs for herself and getting paid, but she was exhausted and unfocused. Lisa's biggest fear was that someone would ask her what she did for a living. She had a hard time defining herself without listing all nine jobs.

Lisa was a parent, teacher, and homeowner and had been successful by creating and maintaining order. It was time to organize her entrepreneurial drive and create a company that could make a difference in women's lives, not just another income stream.

On January 1, 2012, Lisa started a blog called Organize 365. She wasn't sure how it would evolve or generate an income, but she was sure of one thing—she could talk about home organization for the rest of her life.

Establishing Authority

Consistency is a crucial part of building and establishing authority. Lisa started with weekly blog posts. From there she launched the *Organize 365* podcast. One unique thing Lisa did before that launch was she tested her ability to consistently produce a podcast with a 20-episode test podcast. Lisa didn't want to start something in her business that she couldn't keep up consistently.

Consistency in the delivery of your message denotes purposeful planning, commitment, and that you take yourself, your business, and your audience's time seriously.

Next to consistency, you have to get your hands dirty. Nothing will help you shape your message and make your business profitable faster than the one-on-one service experience. It doesn't matter how much you read, practice, or improve yourself, when you can take those skills and help someone else do the same in their lives, that is truly magical.

Three Things to Grow Business Effectively

1. Blogging and podcasting are the two biggest time investments Lisa makes in her business that have the biggest impact on the growth of Organize 365. Lisa spends the majority of her time and mental energy on creating unique, motivational, thought-provoking content to move her audience to action.

2. Lisa's second marketing strategy is to increase the distribution of her posts or podcasts through social sharing, live video, podcast interviews, a weekly newsletter email, and online conversations.

Remember, **when you say "yes" to something**, you're instantly **saying "no" to something else.**

The *Organize 365* podcast is just the beginning of the conversation. Lisa loves hearing her audience's feedback and their ideas of how to organize a space or increase productivity. Often their interaction will create a follow-up podcast, product, or refinement of her message.

3. Lisa uses one-page downloadable printables and seasonal challenges to grow her email list. There is a seasonality to home organization. The week between Christmas and New Year's is a big time for decluttering. January 1 has many Googling "how to get organized." Similarly, back to school, spring-cleaning, holiday preparations, and moving are all events where home organization resources are sought out.

By making an editorial calendar, Lisa can plan out her content around these natural organization seasons and create value-added bonuses and visually appealing full-color printables to help her audience get the information they need when they need it.

Most Profitable Monetization

Lisa's 100 Day Home Organization Program is an online complete home organization program that motivates, inspires, and practically walks homeowners through organizing their entire home with daily 15-minute activities.

In her first four years in business Lisa grew her understanding of the home organization needs of each generation. Since launching this program in December 2015, the 100 Day Home Organization Program has been tested, modified, and enhanced. Lisa's commitment to this program and the three seasonal launches each year have improved the program, her message, and her profitability.

Here's what Lisa had to say about being a YOUPRENEUR:

As my business grows, it is getting harder and harder to find online entrepreneurs who are growing their business with the same intensity and drive I have. I'm not a spring chicken. As a 45-year-old woman, I want to learn and grow with other like-minded business owners who are looking to create businesses like Organize 365 that will be around in 25 years.

The monthly mastermind calls with Chris keep me current in online business trends with the focus being on solid business skills. Youpreneur members are business builders, not people looking to get rich quick. They are supportive, encouraging, and the first place I look to partner and hire to help me grow my business.

CONCLUSION

I T's time to end... with the beginning in mind.

When you build, market, and monetize exactly as I've shown you throughout the pages of this book, you'll be well on your way to a future-proof business as a Youpreneur.

How do I know? Because I'm living proof of it all, right now.

In my own endeavors, I've committed fully to this method of business building, and I've been blown away by how much better it works than any other approach I've tried since the beginning of my own entrepreneurial journey.

Since building MY Youpreneur ecosystem, I've seen my audience grow by tens of thousands, I've published a bestselling book, I've spoken live on stages all over the world, and I've had the honor of serving the type of people I've always known were out there.

People like me. People like YOU.

I've also been privileged to coach literally thousands of student entrepreneurs through this process as part of my You-preneur Mastermind Community. It's because of their success that I know how well and reliably these steps can work for you, regardless of what niche you're in or the type of business you're trying to build.

I encourage you to open your eyes to what's TRULY possible for Youpreneurs who embrace and build on the principles I've shared with you.

If you want to start a business that is immune to the changing whims of technology, industry, politics, and trends, *you can do it* as a Youpreneur.

If you want to become a trusted authority in your market, *you can do it* as a Youpreneur.

If you want to write a book, become a paid speaker, or travel the world serving your customers, *you can do it* as a Youpreneur.

There is no limit to what you can do when you're building, marketing, and monetizing as a personal brand entrepreneur. As your expertise grows, so does your audience. As your interests and pursuits evolve, so does your audience. They grow with you, and you with them, in a limitless cycle of service and generosity.

It's a truly beautiful way to work and serve the world.

RESOURCES

THE following is a complete rundown of important websites, services, software, and solutions that'll make the task of building The Business of You much easier. Some have been mentioned throughout the book, and some I've added here for good measure.

Your first resource is **my personal website**. It's where you'll find hundreds of blog posts, podcast episodes, and videos that'll help you on your entrepreneurial journey. Be sure to hop on my email list when you're there, so you can keep up to date with all the new content that I publish, our live events, my speaking schedule, and other additional projects.

*Head to **ChrisDucker.com** and get started, for free, today!*

The second resource is the **Youpreneur Mastermind Community.** This is the place to be if you want to build a profitable, future-proof business around your experience and those you want to serve. There's nowhere else like it anywhere.

Whether you're just starting out, or if you've been working hard on your personal brand and online platform for a while, the Youpreneur Mastermind Community will help you take everything you're doing to the next level.

With an ever-expanding acceleration library, live master-mind calls, and thriving community forums—where you'll get the feedback, advice, and virtual high-fives we all need—the community is the perfect place for anyone wanting to take their business to a whole new level.

*Visit **Youpreneur.com** for more info and I'll see you on the inside!*

Below (in no particular order), I've broken additional resources up into the three main categories from the book, namely Building, Marketing, and Monetizing, and added a one-sentence explanation for each.

Building

Unsplash.com & Pexels.com Free images to use with your blog posts, social media images, and more.

PickFu.com Brilliant tool to use to come up with website tag-lines, book titles, product names, and more. So easy to use, too.

CrowdfireApp.com Manage your followers on Twitter and Instagram, do targeted following and unfollowing, and schedule posts in advance.

Canva.com Drag-and-drop, cloud-based graphic design software you can use to create professional looking images and artwork for social media.

PlagiarismChecker.com Check written content for duplicated content online—it's important to be original, right?!

ChrisDucker.com/Bluehost Use this special link to get a discounted rate from Bluehost, the company I suggest first-timers check out for their web hosting.

ChrisDucker.com/WPEngine Time to take it up a notch? WPEngine is the best hosting company on the planet for serious online entrepreneurs. I love everything about them.

CoSchedule.com Brilliant content calendar software for Wordpress users.

ConvertKit.com/Youpreneur My preferred and highly recommended email marketing provider. Use that special link and get a full month's service for FREE!

Marketing

MeetEdgar.com Schedule and manage all your social media posts in advance, from one dashboard. This is the tool we use at Youpreneur HQ.

SlideShare.net Online presentation (PowerPoint, Keynote) sharing platform. Perfect for repurposing your blog, video, and podcast content.

LeadPages.com This landing page software makes it easy to integrate different pages, forms, and more into your existing website and mailing list.

PowerUpPodcasting.com The definitive course on how to create, market, and monetize a podcast, by Pat Flynn.

Monetizing

"1000 True Fans" Essential reading by Kevin Kelly. How many subscribers do you really need to succeed?

SurveyMonkey.com Simple to use, yet a powerful tool that'll help you validate your ideas, to make sure you hit the ground running.

ChrisDucker.com/SamCart My preferred shopping cart software. Very easy to setup, it'll help you get started with selling your products and services online fast. Free trial with my link, too.

Teachable.com Great place to build out your online courses if you don't want to host them on your own servers. Easy to use and customizable.

Growth

Inside the Youpreneur Mastermind Community we have one additional track to our Youpreneur Roadmap, which comes after the "Monetizing" stage.

It's simply entitled GROWTH.

The following resources will help you expand your business, your mindset, and your bank balance even further, with a focus on long-term growth.

VirtualStaffFinder.com Sooner or later, you'll need help. VSF can help you find top-quality, experienced virtual staff to help you run, support, and grow your business. Author owned and operated.

Slack.com Quite frankly, the best collaboration tool on the planet. Nothing comes close. We use it every day at the Youpreneur HQ and it boosts everyone's productivity.

ChooseMuse.com This meditation app has helped bring a little calm to the entrepreneurial storm for me and many others. I love the real-time "scores" you get after each session.

Sleep Smarter This brilliant book by Shawn Stevenson is required reading for every entrepreneur wanting to be the best version of themselves possible.

Profit First In his bestselling book, Mike Michalowicz reveals ridiculously simple strategies to maximize profits and minimize silliness in your business.

The Miracle Morning This international bestselling book by Hal Elrod changed a whole lot about how I tackle the most important part of the day—the start of it.

Will It Fly? This *Wall Street Journal* bestselling book from Pat Flynn will help take your idea validation to a whole new level, minimizing time lost to startup mistakes.

Visit the Companion Website

Lastly, don't forget to spend some time on the companion website for this book. You'll find all the templates, process blueprints, links to resources (including those above and more that will be added in the future), additional content, interviews with successful Youpreneurs, and much, much more.

As a reader of the book you have instant access to everything for FREE at:

Youpreneur.com/ReadersOnly

Are YOU Ready to Rise?

I want you to be part of this movement. I want you to realize every dream you have for your business and your family, and I want to be with you every step of the way.

Reading this book was your first step, and I congratulate you on getting to this stage. Taking the next step is as easy as visiting the link below, where you'll find the Youpreneur "Next Step" Assessment.

Specifically designed to help you determine where you're currently at in the *Build, Market, Monetize* process, and how I can best support your growth going forward, this quick-to-complete assessment will be the game-changer you need to kick-start your Youpreneur journey.

Complete the assessment—it will only take you a few minutes.

Visit **Youpreneur.com/NextStep** today, and let's get started.

GRATITUDE

YOU might think that this being my second book, things were a lot easier this time around. If you thought that, you'd be wrong. It would've been impossible for this book to see the light of day without a collection of incredible individuals contributing and helping behind the scenes.

In particular, I'd like to thank the following:

My wife, Ercille, for continuing to inspire me to chase down my entrepreneurial dreams and consistently helping me see the importance of always providing value in my work. I'm in awe of your generosity and never-ending love and support.

My children: CJ, Chloe, Charlie, and Cassie. You are all I need to continue to wake up every day, ready to serve and provide. My legacy is YOU and everything you will achieve in life. I love you more than anything.

Lewis Howes, for his long-lasting friendship and for writing a brilliant foreword to the book. You inspire me daily to achieve my own level of greatness.

Carrie Wilkerson, Amy Schmittauer, Janet Murray, Anissa Holmes, Lisa Woodruff, Callie Willows, Jay Baer, Jeff Goins,

Mike Morrison, Jeff McMahon, and Roger Edwards for agreeing to share their own personal brand business journeys as case studies in the book. You're all living proof that the world needs us Youpreneurs.

My editor, Chantel Hamilton of Afterwords Communications. You've kept me in line, minimized my rambling, controlled my British-isms, and made me sound smarter than ever.

My incredible team at the Youpreneur HQ. Every one of you has contributed to this book in some way, shape, or form. You're awesome.

My best buddy, and brother from another mother, Pat Flynn for his non-stop thoughtfulness and unwavering support. Having you and your family in my family's life makes it so much more enjoyable and unforgettable.

Anyone and everyone that's ever subscribed to my blog, attended one of my live events, commented on one of my YouTube videos, reviewed my podcast on iTunes, sent me a message on social media, or simply emailed me with a quick "Thank you" message. I'll never take your attention for granted.

And finally, to each and every Youpreneur Mastermind Community member—past, present, andW those that join us in the future. Your support, praise, and appreciation mean more to me than I could ever put into words. You remind me DAILY just what I was put on this planet to do. I promise I'll do my best to never let you down.

INDEX OF KEY TERMS

Get your free copy of the 'Official Companion Workbook'

Before you go... I'd like to invite you to review *Rise of the Youpreneur* on whatever website you purchased it from.

As an author, there is genuinely nothing more I enjoy than reading reviews on Amazon and other book-selling websites from those who have enjoyed the book.

As an extra way of saying 'thank you' for posting a review, I've put together an exclusive companion workbook that you can print out and go through as you plan your Youpreneur Ecosystem and much more—it'll speed up the entire learning and action-taking process for you, from start to finish.

All you need to do to get your free companion workbook is simply email a copy of your review (take a photo of your computer screen if you have to!) to **youpreneur@chrisducker.com** and we'll reply, attaching the workbook directly, so you can get to work straightaway.

Thanks in advance for your support,

CHRIS

ABOUT THE AUTHOR

Chris Ducker is the bestselling author of *Virtual Freedom* and founder of Youpreneur.com—the entrepreneurial mastermind community that helps experts become the go-to leader in their market.

A true entrepreneur at heart, he has built several businesses since venturing into the world of entrepreneurship in 2004, which today collectively house over 450 full-time employees and generate a multi-seven-figure annual revenue.

A highly sought-after keynote speaker, trusted international business mentor, blogger, and podcaster, Chris is featured regularly in *Entrepreneur, Inc., Success, Forbes, The Huffington Post*, and several other key media outlets.

Relishing the opportunity to help build strategies for other passionate entrepreneurs that want to grow their businesses in productive and effective ways, Chris hosts several live events each year, including the annual Youpreneur Summit in London.

Chris recently relocated back to the UK after many years based in the Philippines, and now lives with his wife and four children in Cambridgeshire.

You can reach out to him directly on Twitter @ChrisDucker, or visit his personal website at ChrisDucker.com.

9 781999 857943